Turn Your Home Into Your Favorite Southwestern Restaurant

With its fresh ingredients, bold flavors and endless versatility, it's no wonder Southwestern cuisine is finding its way into more and more kitchens. Now *Taste of Home Southwestern Made Easy* puts 211 of these mouth-watering specialties within reach of today's home cook.

Featuring both authentic staples and new flavor twists, *Southwestern Made Easy* guarantees that families can enjoy the restaurant-style fare they crave without leaving the comfort of their own home or spending lots of money. Six enticing chapters—Salsas, Snacks & Beverages; Soups, Chili & Stews; Sides & Salads; Main Dishes; Southwestern Specialties; and Desserts—pack in each of your all-time south-of-the-border favorites.

Get your fiesta off to a great start with a bowl of crunchy tortilla chips and Chunky Cucumber Salsa (p. 7), a platter of Seafood Nachos (p. 19) and a pitcher of refreshing Sangria (p. 10).

To satisfy appetites of grande proportion, turn to heartier choices such as Southwestern Meat and Potato Stew (p. 32), Cheesy Chimichangas (p. 60), Chicken Quesadillas (p. 66), Beef-Stuffed Sopaipillas (p. 72) and Texas Style Lasagna (p. 88).

When something lighter is in order, or you just need to round out a meal, Beef Fajita Salad (p. 39), Salsa Corn Cakes (p. 43) and Spicy Spanish Rice (p. 51) won't disappoint! Top it all off with creamy Fantastic Flan Pie (p. 95), Mexican Fried Ice Cream (p. 103) and other irresistible treats for dessert.

Thanks to everyday ingredients, step-by-step instructions, handy cooking tips and full-color photos, creating the vibrant and colorful dishes you love couldn't be easier.

taste of home SOUTHWESTERN MADE EASY

Editor:	Sara Lancaster
Art Director:	Rudy Krochalk
Layout Designers:	Nancy Novak, Kathy Crawford
Content Production Supervisor:	Julie Wagner
Proofreader:	Linne Bruskewitz
Editorial Assistant:	Barb Czysz
Recipe Asset Management System:	Coleen Martin (Manager), Sue A. Jurack (Specialist)
Indexer:	Jean Duerst
Food Director:	Diane Werner
Test Kitchen Manager:	Karen Scales
Recipe Editors:	Mary King, Christine Rukavena
Studio Photographers:	Rob Hagen (Senior), Dan Roberts, Jim Wieland, Lori Foy
Food Stylists:	Sarah Thompson (Senior), Kaitlyn Basasie, Alynna Malson (Assistant)
Set Stylists:	Jennifer Bradly Vent (Senior), Stephanie Marchese (Senior), Melissa Haberman, Dee Dee Jacq
Photo Studio Coordinator:	Kathleen Swaney
Senior Editor/Books:	Mark Hagen
Creative Director:	Ardyth Cope
Vice President, Executive Editor/Books:	Heidi Reuter Lloyd
Senior Vice President/Editor in Chief:	Catherine Cassidy
President, Food & Entertaining:	Suzanne M. Grimes
President and Chief Executive Officer:	Mary G. Berner
Cover Photography:	Dan Roberts (Photographer), Jennifer Bradley Vent (Set Stylist), Susan Breckenridge (Food Stylist)

©2009 Reiman Media Group, Inc.
5400 S. 60th St.
Greendale, WI 53129

International Standard Book Number (10): 0-89821-630-3
International Standard Book Number (13): 978-0-89821-630-1
Library of Congress Control Number: 2008931531

Pictured on front cover: Pepper Steak Quesadillas (p. 63), Bean and Pineapple Salsa (p. 21), Mexican Fried Ice Cream (p. 103)

Pictured on back cover: Taquitos with Salsa, (p. 6), Green Chili Stew, (p. 23), Fantastic Flan Pie, (p. 95)

SOPA DE TORTILLA, P. 28

PORK FAJITA KABOBS, P. 66

PEACH CHIMMIES, P. 101

Table of Contents

Salsas, Snacks & Beverages

PEPPY PEACH SALSA, P. 16

SOPES

SOPES

Similar to tortillas, sopes are made with a traditional Mexican flour called masa harina. Enjoy making your own!
—Taste of Home Test Kitchen, Greendale, Wisconsin

2	cups masa harina
1	teaspoon salt
1-1/3	cups warm water
1-1/2	cups shredded cooked chicken breast
1	cup salsa, *divided*
1/4	cup lard
1	cup refried beans
1	cup shredded lettuce
1/2	cup crumbled queso fresco

In a small bowl, combine masa harina and salt; stir in water. Knead until mixture forms a ball. Divide dough into 16 portions; shape into balls and cover with plastic wrap.

Working between two sheets of plastic wrap, press four balls into 3-1/2-in. circles. On an ungreased griddle, cook dough circles over medium-low heat for 1-2 minutes or until bottoms are lightly set. Turn and cook 2 minutes longer. Remove from the heat; quickly pinch edge of circles to form a 1/2-in. rim. Return to the griddle; cook for 2 minutes longer or until bottoms are lightly browned. Remove to wire racks; cover. Repeat process with the remaining dough.

In a small saucepan, combine chicken and 1/2 cup salsa. Cook over medium-low heat until heated through, stirring occasionally. In a large skillet, melt lard. Cook sopes over medium-high heat for 2 minutes on each side or until crisp and lightly browned. Remove sopes to paper towels to drain.

To assemble, layer each sope with refried beans, chicken mixture and remaining salsa. Sprinkle with lettuce and queso fresco. Serve immediately. **Yield: 16 servings.**

REFRESHING LEMON-LIME DRINK

Here is a lighter version of the famous margarita—without the alcohol. Bursting with a refreshing blend of lemon and lime, this beverage is perfect for get-togethers on hot summer days or on a buffet of Mexican favorites.
—Lisa Castillo, Bourbonnais, Illinois

1	can (12 ounces) frozen limeade concentrate, thawed
2/3	cup frozen lemonade concentrate, thawed
1	teaspoon orange extract
1-1/2	cups water
6	cups chilled diet lemon-lime soda
1	medium lemon, sliced
1	medium lime, sliced

In a large container, combine the limeade and lemonade concentrates and orange extract. Stir in water.

Just before serving, stir in lemon-lime soda. Serve over ice. Garnish with lemon and lime slices. **Yield: 3 quarts (12 servings, 1 cup per serving).**

REFRESHING LEMON-LIME DRINK

TAQUITOS WITH SALSA

SOUTHWESTERN ONION RINGS

These light, crispy onion rings are sliced thin and spiced just right with garlic powder, cayenne pepper, chili powder and cumin. My family likes nibbling on them alongside grilled burgers. They are even tasty as leftovers.

—Tamra Kriedeman, Enderlin, North Dakota

 2   large sweet onions
2-1/2   cups buttermilk
 2   eggs
 3   tablespoons water
1-3/4   cups all-purpose flour
 2   teaspoons salt
 2   teaspoons chili powder
 1   to 2 teaspoons cayenne pepper
 1   teaspoon sugar
 1   teaspoon garlic powder
 1   teaspoon ground cumin

Oil for frying

Cut onions into 1/4-in. slices; separate into rings. Place in a large bowl; cover with buttermilk and soak for 30 minutes, stirring twice.

In a shallow dish, beat eggs and water. In another shallow bowl, combine the flour, salt, chili powder, cayenne, sugar, garlic powder and cumin. Drain onion rings; dip in egg mixture, then roll in flour mixture.

In an electric skillet or deep-fat fryer, heat 1 in. of oil to 375°. Fry onion rings, a few at a time, for 1 to 1-1/2 minutes on each side or until golden brown. Drain on paper towels. **Yield: 8 servings.**

TAQUITOS WITH SALSA

Our staff jazzed up store-bought quesadilla rolls from the freezer section with a spicy salsa that's a breeze to create. Try serving the combo as an appetizer, snack or quick dinner.

—Taste of Home Test Kitchen, Greendale, Wisconsin

 2   packages (9 ounces *each*) frozen steak quesadilla rolls
 1   jar (16 ounces) lime-garlic salsa
 1   can (10 ounces) diced tomatoes and green chilies, drained
 2   green onions, thinly sliced
 2   tablespoons minced fresh parsley
 2   tablespoons minced fresh cilantro
 2   teaspoons minced garlic
1/2   teaspoon onion salt
1/2   teaspoon pepper

Prepare quesadilla rolls according to package directions for microwave cooking. Meanwhile, for salsa, combine the remaining ingredients in a small bowl. Serve with quesadilla rolls. **Yield: 1 dozen (2-1/2 cups salsa).**

SOUTHWESTERN ONION RINGS

CHUNKY CUCUMBER SALSA

CHUNKY CUCUMBER SALSA

Although this may sound like an "interesting" grouping of flavors, it has never let me down. People always try to guess the secret ingredient...it's mango!

—Sarah Lubner, Milwaukee, Wisconsin

3	medium cucumbers, peeled and coarsely chopped
1	medium mango, coarsely chopped
1	cup frozen corn, thawed
1	medium sweet red pepper, coarsely chopped
1	small red onion, coarsely chopped
1	jalapeno pepper, finely chopped
3	garlic cloves, minced
2	tablespoons white wine vinegar
1	tablespoon minced fresh cilantro
1	teaspoon salt
1/2	teaspoon sugar
1/4	to 1/2 teaspoon cayenne pepper

In a large bowl, combine all the ingredients. Cover and refrigerate for 2-3 hours before serving. **Yield: 4 cups.**

Editor's Note: When cutting hot peppers, disposable gloves are recommended. Avoid touching your face.

MICROWAVE TEXAS NACHOS

Ideal for two, these easy nachos are great for a light luncheon or late-night snack. If you would like, substitute chicken for the spicy pork sausage.

—Carl Dahlgren, Fort Worth, Texas

2	ounces uncooked chorizo *or* 2 ounces bulk spicy pork sausage
1	garlic clove, minced
1/4	cup refried beans
2	cups tortilla chips
1/2	cup shredded Colby-Monterey Jack cheese
1/2	cup shredded lettuce
1	small tomato, seeded and diced
3	tablespoons chopped onion
1/4	cup sour cream
1/4	cup guacamole
2	tablespoons sliced jalapeno pepper

In a small skillet, cook sausage and garlic over medium heat until meat is no longer pink; drain. In a microwave-safe dish, combine the sausage mixture and beans. Cover and microwave on high for 1-2 minutes or until heated through; stir.

Place the tortilla chips on a microwave-safe serving plate; sprinkle with cheese. Heat, uncovered, on high for 1 minute or until cheese is melted. Crumble sausage mixture over chips and cheese. Top with the lettuce, tomato, onion, sour cream, guacamole and jalapeno. Serve immediately. **Yield: 2 servings.**

MICROWAVE TEXAS NACHOS

SALSA VERDE

SALSA VERDE

This flavorful salsa created by our home economists is delicious with tortilla chips, but also just as tasty served on tacos and grilled meats and other Southwestern favorites.

—Taste of Home Test Kitchen, Greendale, Wisconsin

    1   pound tomatillos, husks removed and rinsed
    3   to 4 serrano peppers, stems removed
  1/4   cup chopped onion
    4   tablespoons chopped fresh cilantro, *divided*
    2   garlic cloves, peeled
    1   teaspoon salt

In an ungreased skillet, cook tomatillos over medium heat for 10 minutes or until tender and browned, turning frequently. Cool tomatillos on a wire rack. For a milder flavor, remove veins and seeds from serrano peppers; finely chop peppers.

In a food processor or blender, combine the tomatillos, peppers, onion, 2 tablespoons cilantro, garlic and salt; cover and pulse just until mixture is coarsely pureed. Transfer to a serving bowl; sprinkle with remaining cilantro. Refrigerate until serving. **Yield: 2-1/4 cups.**

Editor's Note: *When cutting hot peppers, disposable gloves are recommended. Avoid touching your face.*

STUFFED BANANA PEPPERS

I received this recipe from a customer while working at my sister's produce market. The peppers can be made a day in advance, making them great for get-togethers.

—Cathy Kidd, Medora, Indiana

    2   packages (8 ounces *each*) cream cheese, softened
    1   envelope ranch salad dressing mix
    1   cup (4 ounces) finely shredded cheddar cheese
    5   bacon strips, cooked and crumbled
    8   mild banana peppers (about 6 inches long), halved lengthwise and seeded

In a small bowl, combine the cream cheese, salad dressing mix, cheese and bacon until blended. Pipe or stuff into pepper halves. Cover and refrigerate until serving. Cut into 1-1/4-in. pieces. **Yield: 8-10 servings.**

EASY CHEESY NACHOS

Crunchy chips are topped with warm canned chili and melted cheese, then sprinkled with chopped tomato and onion for a satisfying and convenient snack.

—Laura Jirasek, Howell, Michigan

    1   package (14-1/2 ounces) tortilla chips
    2   cans (15 ounces *each*) chili without beans
    1   pound process cheese (Velveeta), cubed
    4   green onions, sliced
    1   medium tomato, chopped

Divide chips among six plates; set aside. In a saucepan, warm chili until heated through. Meanwhile, in another saucepan, heat cheese over medium-low heat until melted, stirring frequently. Spoon chili over chips; drizzle with cheese. Sprinkle with onions and tomato. **Yield: 6 servings.**

EASY CHEESY NACHOS

HOT MEXICAN DIP

This hearty dip will disappear in a flash at your next gathering. Green chilies, taco sauce and chili powder add zip to the appetizing blend of ground turkey, refried beans, cheese and zesty seasonings.

—Heather O'Neill, Dudley, Massachusetts

1	pound lean ground turkey
1-1/2	teaspoons chili powder
1	teaspoon onion powder
1/4	teaspoon salt
1	can (16 ounces) refried beans
1	can (4 ounces) chopped green chilies
3/4	cup taco sauce
2	cups (8 ounces) shredded Mexican cheese blend, *divided*
1	cup (8 ounces) sour cream
1/3	cup chopped green onions

Tortilla chips

Crumble turkey into a large nonstick skillet. Cook turkey over medium heat until no longer pink; drain. Add the chili powder, onion powder and salt; set aside. In a 13-in. x 9-in. baking dish coated with cooking spray, layer the beans, turkey mixture, green chilies, taco sauce and 1-1/2 cups Mexican cheese blend.

Cover and bake at 400° for 25-30 minutes or until cheese is melted and bubbles around edges. Cool for 5 minutes. Spread sour cream on top; sprinkle with green onions and remaining cheese. Serve with tortilla chips. **Yield: 15 servings.**

WARM BLACK BEAN DIP

Cumin and chili powder pack a flavorful punch into this chunky bean dip, which is served warm. It's a great make-ahead dish for any kind of party or get-together.

—Lynda Cavanaugh, De Forest, Wisconsin

1	small onion, chopped
2	garlic cloves, minced
1	teaspoon canola oil
1	can (15 ounces) black beans, rinsed and drained
1/2	cup diced fresh tomato
1/3	cup picante sauce
1/2	teaspoon ground cumin
1/2	teaspoon chili powder
1/4	cup shredded reduced-fat Mexican cheese blend *or* cheddar cheese
1/4	cup minced fresh cilantro
1	tablespoon lime juice

Tortilla chips

In a large nonstick skillet, saute onion and garlic in oil until tender. Add the beans; mash gently. Stir in the tomato, picante sauce, cumin and chili powder. Cook and stir just until heated through. Remove from heat; stir in cheese, cilantro and lime juice. Serve warm with chips. **Yield: 2 cups.**

WARM BLACK BEAN DIP

Easy Kitchen Tips

When a recipe calls for a clove of garlic and you don't have fresh garlic bulbs on hand, simply substitute 1/4 teaspoon of garlic powder for each clove.

Or the next time you are out shopping, look for convenient jars of fresh minced garlic in the produce section. Substitute 1/2 teaspoon of minced garlic for each clove called for in the recipe.

MOLE POBLANO

This sauce that gets its rich flavor from a blend of chilies, seasonings and Mexican chocolate. Traditionally, the thick sauce is served over poultry.

—Taste of Home Test Kitchen, Greendale, Wisconsin

3	medium tomatoes, coarsely chopped
6	*each* dried ancho, mulato and pasilla chilies, stems and seeds removed
10	tablespoons shortening, *divided*
1/4	cup sesame seeds, toasted
1/4	teaspoon *each* coriander seeds and aniseed, toasted
10	whole peppercorns
4	whole cloves
1	cinnamon stick (1/2 inch)
1/4	cup chopped almonds
1/4	cup salted pumpkin seeds *or* pepitas
3	garlic cloves, peeled
1/4	cup raisins
2	slices French bread (1 inch thick), cubed
8	cups chicken broth, *divided*
2	ounces Mexican chocolate squares, chopped
1/4	teaspoon salt

In an ungreased skillet, cook tomatoes over medium heat for 10 minutes or until browned; set aside. In the same skillet, cook peppers, a few at a time, over medium heat in 4 tablespoons shortening for 20-30 seconds, turning often; drain. Place peppers in a large bowl of hot water; cover and soak for 1 hour.

In a spice grinder, combine sesame seeds, coriander seeds, aniseed, peppercorns, cloves and cinnamon; process until finely ground. Set aside.

In a skillet, cook the almonds, pumpkin seeds and garlic in 4 tablespoons shortening until lightly browned, stirring often. Add raisins; cook and stir for 1-2 minutes or until raisins are plump. Add bread cubes; cook and stir for 2-3 minutes or until crisp. Drain well.

In a blender, combine 1 cup broth and reserved tomatoes; cover and puree. Add seasoning mixture, raisin mixture and 1 cup broth; blend until very thick. Pour into a bowl; set aside.

Place 1-1/2 cups broth in blender. Add peppers, one at a time; process to a thick consistency. In a Dutch oven, melt the remaining shortening over medium heat. Add pepper mixture; cook and stir for 10 minutes. Add tomato mixture; cook and stir for 6-8 minutes or until thickened. Add the Mexican chocolate, salt and remaining broth. Simmer, uncovered, for 45 minutes or until mixture reaches desired consistency. Serve sauce with poultry. **Yield: 8-1/2 cups.**

Editor's Note: When cutting hot peppers, disposable gloves are recommended. Avoid touching your face.

MOLE POBLANO

SANGRIA

This fresh, fruity make-ahead beverage is great because the flavors have time to blend together.

—Taste of Home Test Kitchen, Greendale, Wisconsin

1	bottle (750 ml) Zinfandel *or* other fruity red wine
3/4	cup orange juice
1/3	cup unsweetened pineapple juice
1/4	cup superfine sugar
1	medium orange, sliced
1	medium lemon, sliced
1	medium lime, cut into wedges

In a pitcher, combine the wine, orange juice, pineapple juice and sugar; stir until sugar is dissolved. Add fruit, press lightly with a wooden spoon. Refrigerate for 2-4 hours. Serve over ice. **Yield: 5 servings.**

TEXAS CAVIAR

TEXAS CAVIAR

My neighbor gave me a container of this zippy, tangy salsa one Christmas and I had to have the recipe. I fix it regularly for potlucks and get-togethers and never have leftovers. I take copies of the recipe with me whenever I take it.

—Kathy Faris, Lytle, Texas

> 1 can (15-1/2 ounces) black-eyed peas, rinsed and drained
> 3/4 cup chopped sweet red pepper
> 3/4 cup chopped green pepper
> 1 medium onion, chopped
> 3 green onions, chopped
> 1/4 cup minced fresh parsley
> 1 jar (2 ounces) diced pimientos, drained
> 1 garlic clove, minced
> 1 bottle (8 ounces) Italian salad dressing
> Tortilla chips

In a large bowl, combine the peas, peppers, onions, parsley, pimientos and garlic. Pour salad dressing over pea mixture; stir gently to coat. Cover and refrigerate for 24 hours. Serve with tortilla chips. **Yield: 4 cups.**

AVOCADO PINEAPPLE SALSA

This colorful salsa developed by our home economists features the leaves of lovage, which is an aromatic perennial herb. Sweet pineapple balances perfectly with tart lime.

—Taste of Home Test Kitchen, Greendale, Wisconsin

> 1 fresh pineapple, peeled and diced
> 1 medium ripe avocado, peeled and diced
> 1/3 cup finely chopped red onion
> 5 lovage *or* celery leaves, finely chopped
> 1 jalapeno pepper, seeded and chopped
> 3 tablespoons lime juice
> 1 teaspoon grated lime peel
> 1/4 teaspoon salt
> Tortilla chips

In a large bowl, combine the first eight ingredients. Cover and refrigerate for at least 30 minutes before serving. Serve with tortilla chips. **Yield: 5 cups.**

STUFFED JALAPENOS

If you're a fan of jalapeno poppers at restaurants, you're sure to enjoy this homemade version that doesn't call for frying.

—Sandra Thorn, Sonora, California

> 2 jars (11-1/2 ounces *each*) whole jalapeno peppers, drained
> 1 package (8 ounces) cream cheese, softened

Cut a slit along one side of each pepper. Remove seeds; rinse and dry. Fill the inside of each pepper with about 2 teaspoons of cream cheese. **Yield: about 20 appetizers.**

STUFFED JALAPENOS

PEACHY AVOCADO SALSA

PEACHY AVOCADO SALSA

This bright and colorful salsa tastes so fresh, it's a welcome change from the store-bought varieties.

—Shelly Platten, Amherst, Wisconsin

1 can (15-1/4 ounces) sliced peaches, drained and chopped
1 medium ripe avocado, peeled and chopped
1 tablespoon lime juice
2 cups chopped seeded tomatoes
1/4 cup diced onion
2 tablespoons minced fresh cilantro
1 tablespoon cider vinegar
1 to 2 teaspoons seeded chopped jalapeno pepper
1 garlic clove, minced
1/4 teaspoon salt

In a large bowl, combine the peaches, avocado and lime juice. Add the remaining ingredients; lightly toss just until combined. Refrigerate for at least 30 minutes. Serve with tortilla chips, fish or chicken. **Yield: 3 cups.**

Editor's Note: When cutting hot peppers, disposable gloves are recommended. Avoid touching your face.

BAKED CHICKEN NACHOS

Here's a colorful party appetizer that's delicious and so simple. Rotisserie chicken keeps it quick, while the seasonings and splash of lime juice lend fantastic flavor.

—Gail Cawsey, Fawnskin, California

2 medium sweet red peppers, diced
1 medium green pepper, diced
3 teaspoons canola oil, *divided*
1 can (15 ounces) black beans, rinsed and drained
1 teaspoon minced garlic
1 teaspoon dried oregano
1/4 teaspoon ground cumin
2-1/4 cups shredded cooked rotisserie chicken (skin removed)
4-1/2 teaspoons lime juice
1/8 teaspoon salt
1/8 teaspoon pepper
7-1/2 cups tortilla chips
8 ounces pepper Jack cheese, shredded
1/4 cup thinly sliced green onions
1/2 cup minced fresh cilantro
1 cup (8 ounces) sour cream
2 to 3 teaspoons diced pickled jalapeno peppers, optional

In a large skillet, saute peppers in 1-1/2 teaspoons oil for 3 minutes or until crisp-tender; transfer to a small bowl. In the same skillet, saute the beans, garlic, oregano and cumin in remaining oil for 3 minutes or until heated through.

Meanwhile, combine the chicken, lime juice, salt and pepper. In a greased 13-in. x 9-in. baking dish, layer half of the tortilla chips, pepper mixture, bean mixture, chicken, cheese, onions and cilantro. Repeat layers.

Bake, uncovered, at 350° for 15-20 minutes or until heated through. Serve with sour cream and pickled jalapenos if desired. **Yield: 16 servings.**

BAKED CHICKEN NACHOS

SOUTHWESTERN SEAFOOD EGG ROLLS

Scallops, shrimp, spicy seasonings and phyllo dough combine to make these unique egg rolls. Assemble them in the morning, refrigerate, then bake as guests arrive. The bites are sure to be a hit with everyone at your gathering.
—Lori Coeling, Hudsonville, Michigan

- 1/4 pound uncooked bay scallops
- 1/4 pound uncooked medium shrimp, peeled and deveined
- 1 teaspoon minced garlic, *divided*
- 2 tablespoons olive oil, *divided*
- 1 large tomato, peeled, seeded and chopped
- 1/4 cup finely chopped onion
- 3 tablespoons minced fresh parsley
- 3 tablespoons minced fresh cilantro *or* additional parsley
- 3/4 teaspoon ground cumin
- 1/2 teaspoon paprika
- 1/4 teaspoon salt
- 1/8 teaspoon pepper
- Dash cayenne pepper
- Dash ground turmeric
- 1/4 cup soft bread crumbs
- 12 sheets phyllo dough, (14 inches x 9 inches)
- 1/2 cup butter, melted

In a large skillet, saute scallops, shrimp and 1/2 teaspoon garlic in 1 tablespoon oil for 2 minutes or until seafood is opaque. With a slotted spoon, remove from the pan and coarsely chop; set aside.

In the same skillet, combine the tomato, onion and remaining garlic and oil; simmer for 5 minutes. Stir in parsley, cilantro, cumin, paprika, salt, pepper, cayenne and turmeric. Simmer, uncovered, until liquid is evaporated, about 5 minutes. Stir in the seafood mixture and the bread crumbs.

Cut the phyllo dough into 14-in. x 4-1/2-in. strips. Cover with a damp towel until ready to use. Lightly brush one strip with butter. Top with another strip; brush with butter. Place a tablespoonful of seafood mixture near one short side; fold in the long sides and roll up. Brush lightly with butter.

Place on a greased baking sheet. Repeat with remaining phyllo and filling. Bake at 375° for 12-15 minutes or until golden brown. **Yield: 2 dozen.**

FROZEN LEMON-BERRY MARGARITAS

FROZEN LEMON-BERRY MARGARITAS

Cool down those hot summer months with this absolutely fantastic margarita. It's slightly icy, thick and perfect on a lazy afternoon. The non-alcoholic version will be a real hit with kids.
—Julie Hieggelke, Grayslake, Illinois

- 6 lime wedges
- 3 tablespoons coarse sugar
- 2/3 cup lemonade concentrate
- 1 cup frozen unsweetened raspberries
- 2 cups ice cubes
- 1 package (16 ounces) frozen sweetened sliced strawberries, slightly thawed
- 1/2 cup frozen blueberries
- 1 tablespoon sugar
- 1/2 cup tequila, optional

Using lime wedges, moisten the rims of six glasses. Set limes aside for garnish. Sprinkle coarse sugar on a plate; hold each glass upside down and dip rim into sugar. Set aside. Discard remaining sugar on plate.

In a blender, combine the lemonade concentrate and raspberries; cover and process until blended. Press mixture through a fine meshed sieve; discard seeds. Return raspberry mixture to blender; add ice, strawberries, blueberries, sugar and tequila if desired. Cover and process until smooth.

Pour into prepared glasses. Garnish with reserved limes. **Yield: 6 servings.**

SOUTHWESTERN EGG ROLLS

I brought these to a church potluck and everybody loved them. The recipe makes a large amount, but there were no leftovers. I also like that the yummy bites freeze well and can be made ahead of time for quick convenience.

—Jacqueline Bower, Washington, Iowa

- 1 pound bulk hot Italian sausage
- 1 can (15 ounces) black beans, rinsed and drained
- 1 can (11 ounces) Mexicorn, drained
- 1 can (10 ounces) diced tomatoes and green chilies, undrained
- 1 package (8.8 ounces) ready-to-serve Spanish rice
- 19 egg roll wrappers

Oil for frying

In a large skillet, cook sausage over medium heat until no longer pink; drain. Stir in the beans, Mexicorn, tomatoes and rice. Bring to a boil. Reduce heat; simmer, uncovered, for 5-10 minutes or until heated through.

Place 1/3 cup sausage mixture in the center of each egg roll wrapper. Fold bottom corner over filling. Fold sides toward center over filling. Moisten remaining corner with water; roll up tightly to seal.

In an electric skillet, heat 1 in. of oil to 375°. Fry egg rolls, two at a time, for 30 seconds on each side. Drain on paper towels. Serve warm. **Yield: 19 egg rolls.**

SOUTHWESTERN EGG ROLLS

FIESTA CRAB DIP

This mild, fresh-tasting crab dip tempts taste buds with a hint of picante zip. We enjoy it in place of salsa.

—Patricia Walls, Aurora, Minnesota

- 1 package (8 ounces) cream cheese, softened
- 1 cup picante sauce
- 1 package (8 ounces) imitation crabmeat, chopped
- 1 cup (4 ounces) shredded cheddar cheese
- 1/3 cup thinly sliced green onions
- 2 tablespoons sliced ripe olives
- 2 tablespoons diced fresh tomato
- 2 tablespoons minced fresh cilantro

Tortilla chips, assorted crackers *or* fresh vegetables

In a large bowl, beat cream cheese and picante sauce until blended. Add the crab, cheese and onions and mix well. Cover and refrigerate until serving. Transfer to a serving bowl. Sprinkle with the olives, tomato and cilantro. Serve with the chips, crackers or vegetables. **Yield: 3 cups.**

PINEAPPLE MANGO SALSA

This fruity medley is wonderful at summer barbecues. Enjoy the unique blend of flavors on crunchy tortilla chips or serve it alongside fish and chicken entrees.

—Mary Gloede, Lakewood, Wisconsin

- 1 cup chopped peeled mango
- 1 cup pineapple tidbits
- 1/2 cup diced sweet red pepper
- 1 plum tomato, seeded and chopped
- 3 tablespoons minced fresh cilantro
- 2 green onions, sliced
- 2 tablespoons lime juice
- 1 tablespoon lemon juice
- 1 jalapeno pepper, finely chopped

Tortilla chips

In a large bowl, combine the first nine ingredients. Cover and refrigerate for 1 hour or until chilled. Serve with tortilla chips. **Yield: 2-2/3 cups.**

Editor's Note: When cutting hot peppers, disposable gloves are recommended. Avoid touching your face.

CALICO CORN SALSA

CALICO CORN SALSA

A friend gave me the recipe for this colorful salsa. When I took it to a luncheon, everyone devoured it. Double the ingredients when you are expecting a larger crowd.

—Jennifer Gardner, Sandy, Utah

1-1/2 cups frozen corn, thawed
1 cup frozen peas, thawed
1/2 teaspoon ground cumin
1/8 teaspoon dried oregano
1 tablespoon olive oil
1 can (15 ounces) black beans, rinsed and drained
1 medium tomato, chopped
1/3 cup chopped red onion
1/4 cup lime juice
1 tablespoon Dijon mustard
1 garlic clove, minced
1/2 teaspoon salt
2 tablespoons minced fresh cilantro
Tortilla chips

In a large bowl, combine the corn and peas. In a nonstick skillet, cook cumin and oregano in oil over medium heat for 2 minutes. Pour over corn mixture; stir to coat evenly. Stir in the beans, tomato and onion.

In a small bowl, whisk the lime juice, mustard, garlic and salt. Stir in cilantro. Pour over corn mixture and stir to coat. Serve with tortilla chips. Refrigerate leftovers. **Yield: 4 cups.**

TACO PINWHEELS

The colorful tomatoes, lettuce and chilies make these bite-size snacks a perfect addition to any appetizer buffet.
—Beverly Matthews, Pasco, Washington

1 package (8 ounces) cream cheese, softened
1 tablespoon taco seasoning
1 can (16 ounces) refried beans
8 flour tortillas (10 inches), room temperature
3 cups shredded lettuce
2 large tomatoes, seeded and finely chopped
2 cans (4 ounces *each*) chopped green chilies
1 cup finely chopped ripe olives
Salsa

In a small bowl, beat cream cheese and taco seasoning until blended. Stir in the refried beans. Spread 3-4 tablespoons over each tortilla. Layer lettuce, tomatoes, chilies and olives down the center of each tortilla; roll up tightly to 2-in. diameter.

Wrap rolled tortillas in plastic wrap and refrigerate for at least 1 hour. Cut each tortilla into 1-in. slices. Serve with salsa. **Yield: about 5 dozen.**

TACO PINWHEELS

CHEDDAR SHRIMP NACHOS

CHEDDAR SHRIMP NACHOS

These fun finger foods served in tortilla chip scoops are just the thing when you're in need of a crowd-pleasing snack.
—Lisa Feld, Grafton, Wisconsin

> 3/4 pound deveined peeled cooked shrimp, chopped
> 1-1/2 cups (6 ounces) shredded cheddar cheese
> 1 can (4 ounces) chopped green chilies, drained
> 1/3 cup chopped green onions
> 1/4 cup sliced ripe olives, drained
> 1/2 cup mayonnaise
> 1/4 teaspoon ground cumin
> 48 tortilla chip scoops

In a large bowl, combine the shrimp, cheese, chilies, onions and olives. Combine the mayonnaise and cumin; add to shrimp mixture and toss to coat. Drop by tablespoonfuls into tortilla scoops. Place on ungreased baking sheets. Bake at 350° for 5-10 minutes or until cheese is melted. Serve warm. **Yield: 4 dozen.**

CONFETTI GUACAMOLE

Whenever I make this colorful guacamole for family parties, I double the recipe because one batch isn't enough!
—Cindy Colley, Othello, Washington

> 2 medium ripe avocados, peeled
> 1 cup frozen corn, thawed
> 1 cup canned black beans, rinsed and drained
> 1 medium tomato, peeled, seeded and diced

> 1/4 cup lemon juice
> 1 tablespoon chopped green onion
> 1 jalapeno pepper, seeded and chopped
> 1/2 to 1 teaspoon minced garlic
> 1/2 teaspoon salt
> Corn *or* tortilla chips

In a bowl, mash avocados. Gently stir in the corn, beans, tomato, lemon juice, onion, jalapeno, garlic and salt. Serve immediately with chips. **Yield: 3-1/2 cups.**

Editor's Note: When cutting hot peppers, disposable gloves are recommended. Avoid touching your face.

PEPPY PEACH SALSA

Garden-fresh salsas are one of my favorite condiments. When I saw a recipe for peach salsa in the newspaper, I couldn't think of anything that sounded better.
—Jennifer Abbott, Moraga, California

> 2 tablespoons lime juice
> 1 tablespoon honey
> 1/2 teaspoon minced garlic
> 1/8 teaspoon ground ginger
> 2 fresh peaches, peeled and diced
> 1/2 green serrano chili pepper, seeded and minced
> 1/2 red serrano chili pepper, seeded and minced
> 1/2 small yellow chili pepper, seeded and minced
> 2 teaspoons minced fresh cilantro
> Tortilla chips

In a small bowl, combine the lime juice, honey, garlic and ginger; let stand for 5 minutes. Stir in the peaches, peppers and cilantro. Serve with chips. Refrigerate leftovers. **Yield: 1-1/4 cups.**

PEPPY PEACH SALSA

JALAPENO POPPERS

After sampling similar poppers at a wedding reception, I went home to create my own recipe. The creamy filling pairs well with the crunchy, spicy peppers. They're great for casual get-togethers any time of the year.

—James Brophy, Feasterville Trevose, Pennsylvania

  2   jars (11-1/2 ounces *each*) jalapeno peppers
  1   package (8 ounces) cream cheese, softened
  1   cup (4 ounces) shredded cheddar cheese
1/4   cup grated Parmesan cheese
  1   tablespoon dried parsley flakes
  2   teaspoons garlic salt
  2   teaspoons paprika
1/4   cup all-purpose flour
  3   eggs
  1   cup crushed cornflakes
1/2   cup dry bread crumbs
Oil for frying
SAUCE:
1/4   cup mayonnaise
1/4   cup prepared Russian salad dressing
  1   teaspoon prepared horseradish
  1   teaspoon dried parsley flakes
1/2   teaspoon pepper
1/4   teaspoon salt
Dash Louisiana-style hot sauce

Select 12-16 large jalapenos from jars; pat dry with paper towels (refrigerate any remaining jalapenos for another use). Remove stems from jalapenos; cut a lengthwise slit on one side. Discard seeds.

In a small mixing bowl, combine the cheeses, parsley, garlic salt and paprika. Pipe or stuff into each pepper.

Place flour in a shallow bowl. In another shallow bowl, lightly beat the eggs.

In a separate bowl, combine cornflakes and bread crumbs. Roll jalapenos in flour, dip in eggs, then roll in crumbs. Dip again in eggs, then roll in crumbs to completely coat.

In an electric skillet, heat 1/4 in. of oil to 375°. Fry peppers, a few at a time, for 30-60 seconds or until lightly browned. Drain on paper towels. In a small bowl, combine sauce ingredients. Serve with warm peppers.
Yield: 12-16 appetizers.

CORN 'N' SQUASH QUESADILLAS

CORN 'N' SQUASH QUESADILLAS

Grilled vegetables give these quesadillas their distinctive flair, while the cumin and jalapeno peppers add a little zip.

—Mildred Sherrer, Fort Worth, Texas

  2   medium ears sweet corn, husks removed
  2   medium yellow summer squash, halved lengthwise
1/2   small sweet onion, cut into 1/4-inch slices
  1   to 2 jalapeno peppers
  1   tablespoon minced fresh basil
1-1/2 teaspoons minced fresh oregano
  1   garlic clove, minced
1/4   teaspoon salt
1/4   teaspoon ground cumin
  6   flour tortillas (8 inches), warmed
  1   cup (4 ounces) shredded Monterey Jack cheese
  1   tablespoon canola oil

Grill corn, covered, over medium heat for 10 minutes; turn. Place squash, onion and jalapenos on grill; cover and cook for 10 minutes, turning once. When cool enough to handle, remove corn from cobs, chop squash and onion, and seed and chop jalapenos. Place in a large bowl.

Stir in basil, oregano, garlic, salt and cumin. Place 1/2 cup filling on one side of each tortilla; sprinkle with cheese. Fold tortillas over filling. On a griddle, cook quesadillas in oil over medium heat for 1-2 minutes on each side. Cut into wedges. **Yield: 6 servings.**

SANTA FE CHEESECAKE

SANTA FE CHEESECAKE

All of my favorite Southwestern ingredients are combined in this savory cheesecake. It looks and tastes fantastic!
—Jean Ecos, Hartland, Wisconsin

1   cup crushed tortilla chips
3   tablespoons butter, melted
2   packages (8 ounces *each*) cream cheese, softened
2   eggs, lightly beaten
2   cups (8 ounces) shredded Monterey Jack cheese
1   can (4 ounces) chopped green chilies, drained
1   cup (8 ounces) sour cream
1   cup chopped sweet yellow pepper
1/2 cup chopped green onions
1/3 cup chopped tomato

In a small bowl, combine tortilla chips and butter; press onto the bottom of a greased 9-in. springform pan. Place on a baking sheet. Bake at 325° for 15 minutes or until lightly browned.

In a large bowl, beat the cream cheese and eggs on low speed just until combined. Stir in Monterey Jack cheese and chilies; pour over crust. Bake for 30-35 minutes or until center is almost set.

Place pan on a wire rack. Spread sour cream over cheesecake. Carefully run a knife around edge of pan to loosen; cool for 1 hour. Refrigerate overnight.

Remove sides of pan just before serving. Garnish with yellow pepper, onions and tomato. Refrigerate leftovers.
Yield: 16-20 servings.

CRAB ASPARAGUS QUESADILLAS

This flavorful combination features fresh asparagus and crabmeat with Mexican flair. The bites make eye-fetching appetizers and can even be served as the main course.
—Curtis Gunnarson, Sycamore, Illinois

4   flour tortillas (8 inches)
2   cups (8 ounces) shredded Mexican cheese blend
1   cup chopped fresh asparagus, cooked
1/2 cup chopped imitation crabmeat
2   tablespoons plus 3/4 cup picante sauce, *divided*
2   teaspoons canola oil
6   tablespoons sour cream
12   large ripe olives, sliced

On two tortillas, layer each with 1/2 cup cheese, 1/2 cup asparagus, 1/4 cup crab, 1 tablespoon picante sauce and remaining cheese. Top with remaining tortillas; press down lightly.

In a skillet coated with cooking spray, cook one quesadilla at a time in oil for 2 minutes on each side or until cheese is melted. Cut each quesadilla into six wedges. Serve with sour cream, sliced olives and the remaining picante sauce.
Yield: 6 servings.

CRAB ASPARAGUS QUESADILLAS

FRESH LIME MARGARITAS

For Frozen Strawberry Margaritas: Follow directions for Frozen Lime Margaritas, except reduce crushed ice to 2 cups and add 2 cups frozen unsweetened strawberries. **Yield: 4 cups.**

SEAFOOD NACHOS

I love seafood and sometimes order the seafood nacho appetizer at our local Mexican restaurant as my entree. I have tried many times to duplicate those tasty morsels at home—this recipe comes close to the original version.

—Linda McKee, Big Prairie, Ohio

30	tortilla chips
1	package (8 ounces) imitation crabmeat, chopped
1/4	cup sour cream
1/4	cup mayonnaise
2	tablespoons finely chopped onion
1/4	teaspoon dill weed
1	cup (4 ounces) shredded cheddar cheese
1/4	cup sliced ripe olives
1/4	teaspoon paprika

Arrange tortilla chips in a single layer on an ungreased baking sheet. In a bowl, combine the crab, sour cream, mayonnaise, onion and dill; spoon about 1 tablespoon onto each chip. Sprinkle with cheese, olives and paprika. Bake at 350° for 6-8 minutes or until cheese is melted. **Yield: 6 servings.**

FRESH LIME MARGARITAS

This basic margarita recipe from our home economists is easy to modify to your tastes...try it frozen or with strawberries.

—Taste of Home Test Kitchen, Greendale, Wisconsin

4	lime wedges
1	tablespoon kosher salt
1/2	cup gold tequila
1/4	cup Triple Sec
1/4	cup lime juice
1/4	cup lemon juice
2	tablespoons superfine sugar
1-1/3	cups crushed ice

Using lime wedges, moisten rim of four glasses. Holding each glass upside down, dip rim into salt; set aside.

In a pitcher, combine the tequila, Triple Sec, lime juice, lemon juice and sugar; stir until sugar is dissolved. Serve in prepared glasses over crushed ice. **Yield: 4 servings.**

Editor's Note:
For Frozen Lime Margaritas: Reduce lemon and lime juices to 2 tablespoons each. Increase the superfine sugar to 1/4 cup and the crushed ice to 4 cups. Add 3/4 cup limeade concentrate. Prepare glasses as directed. In a blender, combine the tequila, Triple Sec, lime juice, lemon juice, limeade concentrate, superfine sugar and crushed ice; cover and process until smooth. **Yield: 5 cups.**

SEAFOOD NACHOS

ENCHILADA MEATBALLS

ENCHILADA MEATBALLS

Before I retired, these tasty treats were very popular during snack time at work. They come together quite easily and are a good way to use up leftover corn bread.

—Mearl Harris, West Plains, Missouri

-   2   cups crumbled corn bread
-   1   can (10 ounces) enchilada sauce, *divided*
-   1/2   teaspoon salt
-   1-1/2   pounds ground beef
-   1   can (8 ounces) tomato sauce
-   1/2   cup shredded Mexican cheese blend

In a large bowl, combine the corn bread, 1/2 cup enchilada sauce and salt. Crumble beef mixture; mix well. Shape into 1-in. balls.

Place meatballs on a greased rack in a shallow baking pan. Bake, uncovered, at 350° for 18-22 minutes or until meat is no longer pink; drain.

Meanwhile, in a small saucepan, heat tomato sauce and remaining enchilada sauce. Drain meatballs; place in a serving dish. Top with sauce and sprinkle with cheese. Serve with toothpicks. **Yield: about 4-1/2 dozen.**

MOCK STRAWBERRY MARGARITAS

These refreshing strawberry smoothies from our home economists pair well with spicy Mexican fare. They are a whimsical addition to any table.

—Taste of Home Test Kitchen, Greendale, Wisconsin

-   6   lime wedges
-   3   tablespoons sugar plus 1/3 cup sugar, *divided*
-   1-1/4   cups water
-   1   can (6 ounces) frozen limeade concentrate, partially thawed
-   1   package (16 ounces) frozen unsweetened strawberries
-   25   ice cubes

Using lime wedges, moisten the rim of six glasses. Set limes aside for garnish. Sprinkle 3 tablespoons sugar on a plate; hold each glass upside down and dip rim into sugar. Set aside. Discard remaining sugar on plate.

In a blender, combine the water, limeade concentrate, strawberries, ice cubes and remaining sugar; cover and blend until smooth. Pour mixture into the prepared glasses. Garnish glasses with reserved limes. Serve immediately. **Yield: 6 servings.**

MOCK STRAWBERRY MARGARITAS

Easy Kitchen Tips

-   *Jazz up frozen beverages with an assortment of fun and festive garnishes.*
-   *Instead of placing lime wedges on the sides of the glasses, skewer a few pineapple chunks and perch the fruit kabobs across the top of the glass.*
-   *Add a colored or curvy straw to make the presentation even more enjoyable.*

LOADED TORTILLAS

I tried out these broiler "pizzas" on my family at lunch one day. My husband and daughter loved them and insisted I send in the recipe. The recipe serves two people, but you can increase the ingredients to make as many as you need.

—Terri Keeney, Greeley, Colorado

2	flour tortillas (7 inches)
1/2	cup refried beans
1/2	cup salsa
1/2	cup shredded part-skim mozzarella cheese
1/4	cup shredded cheddar cheese
1/3	cup real bacon bits
1/4	cup chopped tomato
1/4	cup chopped green onion

Place tortillas on an ungreased baking sheet. Spread with beans and salsa. Top with cheeses, bacon and tomato.

Broil 4 in. from the heat for 4-6 minutes or until cheese is melted and edges of tortillas are lightly browned. Sprinkle with onions. **Yield: 2 servings.**

BEAN AND PINEAPPLE SALSA

The flavors of this unique salsa complement each other very nicely. People are pleasantly surprised every time. I like to serve it over either fish or chicken for a delicious and colorful change.

—Anne Bennett, Delmar, Maryland

1/2	cup canned black beans, rinsed and drained
1/4	cup unsweetened pineapple tidbits, drained
1/4	cup chopped green pepper
1/4	cup chopped sweet red pepper
2	tablespoons finely chopped sweet onion
2	tablespoons chopped green chilies
1/2	to 1 teaspoon chopped seeded jalapeno pepper
1	tablespoon rice vinegar
1-1/2	teaspoons minced fresh cilantro
1/2	teaspoon ground coriander
1/2	teaspoon ground cumin

Tortilla chips

In a small bowl, combine the first 11 ingredients. Refrigerate until serving. Serve with tortilla chips. **Yield: 1-1/4 cups.**

Editor's Note: When cutting hot peppers, disposable gloves are recommended. Avoid touching your face.

GRILLED CORN SALSA

GRILLED CORN SALSA

Lime juice lends a tartness to this vibrant medley—a mixture of corn, sweet red pepper, red onion and jalapeno peppers. With its great grilled flavor, this chunky dip is perfect for summer gatherings and patio parties.

—Lorie Fiock, Warren, Indiana

6	medium ears sweet corn
3	teaspoons canola oil, *divided*
1	large sweet red pepper, quartered and seeded
1/2	cup finely chopped red onion
2	medium jalapeno pepper, seeded and chopped
1/4	cup lime juice
1/4	teaspoon salt

Tortilla chips

Remove husks from corn; brush corn and sweet red pepper with 2 teaspoons oil. Coat grill rack with cooking spray before starting the grill.

Prepare grill for indirect heat. Grill corn, covered, over indirect medium heat for 20-25 minutes or until tender, turning often. Grill red pepper over indirect medium heat for 5 minutes on each side or until tender. Cool.

Cut corn from cobs and dice the sweet red pepper; transfer to a large bowl. Stir in the onion, jalapenos, lime juice, salt and remaining oil; toss to coat. Serve with tortilla chips. **Yield: 3 cups.**

Soups, Chili & Stews

SOPA DE TORTILLA, P. 28

TEXAS CORN CHOWDER

GREEN CHILI STEW

This stew is much heartier than most—and very tasty, too. People especially enjoy the zesty broth and the generous amounts of tender beef. They frequently request second helpings of this colorful meal-in-a-bowl.

—Jacqueline Thompson, Lawrenceville, Georgia

2	pounds beef stew meat, cut into 1-inch cubes
2	medium onions, chopped
2	tablespoons canola oil
1	can (15 ounces) pinto beans, rinsed and drained
1	can (14-1/2 ounces) diced tomatoes, undrained
2	cans (4 ounces *each*) chopped green chilies
1	cup water
3	beef bouillon cubes
1	garlic clove, minced
1	teaspoon sugar
1/2	teaspoon salt, optional
1/4	teaspoon pepper

Shredded cheddar *or* Monterey Jack cheese, optional

In a large skillet, brown beef and onions in oil; drain. Transfer to a 5-qt. slow cooker. Combine the beans, tomatoes, chilies, water, bouillon, garlic, sugar, salt if desired and pepper; pour over beef. Cover and cook on low for 7-8 hours or until beef is tender. Sprinkle with cheese if desired. **Yield: 8 servings.**

TEXAS CORN CHOWDER

This recipe has been a family favorite for years. The jalapeno pepper adds the right amount of zip and color!

—Mildred Sherrer, Fort Worth, Texas

1/4	cup chopped onion
1	tablespoon butter
1	tablespoon all-purpose flour
1	cup diced peeled potato (1 medium)
1	cup water
1	chicken bouillon cube
1	cup fresh *or* frozen corn
1	to 2 teaspoons finely chopped jalapeno *or* green chilies
2	cups milk
1/4	teaspoon garlic salt
1/8	teaspoon pepper

Dash paprika

In a large saucepan, saute onion in butter until tender. Stir in flour. Add the potato, water and bouillon; bring to a boil. Reduce heat; cover and simmer for 7-10 minutes or until potato is tender. Add the corn, jalapeno, milk and seasonings. Cover and simmer for 15 minutes. Ladle into bowls and serve. **Yield: 2 servings.**

Editor's Note: When cutting hot peppers, disposable gloves are recommended. Avoid touching your face.

GREEN CHILI STEW

TEXAS STEW

I love to experiment with many different types of recipes. Now, I find myself relying on family-friendly ones more and more, like this hearty stew. It makes a wonderful main dish.

—Kim Balstad, Lewisville, Texas

- 1 can (15-1/2 ounces) hominy, drained
- 1 can (15-1/4 ounces) whole kernel corn, drained
- 1 can (15 ounces) sliced carrots, drained
- 1 can (15 ounces) sliced potatoes, drained
- 1 can (15 ounces) ranch-style *or* chili beans, undrained
- 1 can (14-1/2 ounces) diced tomatoes, undrained
- 1 cup water
- 1 beef bouillon cube
- 1/2 teaspoon garlic powder

Chili powder to taste

Dash Worcestershire sauce

Dash hot pepper sauce

- 1-1/2 pounds ground beef
- 1 medium onion, chopped

In a 5-qt. slow cooker, combine the first 12 ingredients. In a skillet, cook beef and onion over medium heat until meat is no longer pink; drain.

Transfer beef and onions to the slow cooker; mix well. Cover and cook on high for 4 hours or until heated through. **Yield: 10-12 servings.**

TEXAS STEW

SOUTHWESTERN CHICKEN SOUP

SOUTHWESTERN CHICKEN SOUP

The spices in this soup really lend it a delicious kick. This recipe is easily doubled and freezes well, too.

—Anne Smithson, Cary, North Carolina

- 1 can (32 ounces) reduced-sodium chicken broth plus 1 can (14-1/2 ounces) reduced-sodium chicken broth
- 1 can (14-1/2 ounces) crushed tomatoes, undrained
- 1 can (14-1/2 ounces) diced tomatoes, undrained
- 1 pound boneless skinless chicken breast, cut into 1/2-inch cubes
- 1 large onion, chopped
- 1/3 cup minced fresh cilantro
- 1 can (4 ounces) chopped green chilies
- 1 garlic clove, minced
- 1 teaspoon chili powder
- 1 teaspoon ground cumin
- 1/2 teaspoon dried oregano
- 1/4 teaspoon cayenne pepper
- 3 cups frozen corn, thawed

Tortilla chips

- 1 cup (4 ounces) shredded reduced-fat cheddar *or* Mexican cheese blend

In a large saucepan, combine the first 12 ingredients. Bring to a boil. Reduce heat; cover and simmer for 1 hour. Add corn; cook 10 minutes longer. Top each serving with tortilla chips; sprinkle with cheese. **Yield: 8 servings.**

TACO SOUP

I first sampled this soup when I was camping with some friends. After one taste, I just had to have the recipe. It's easy to whip up when you need to feed a crowd or prepare a dish for a group supper but don't have a lot of time to cook.

—Jane Ficiur, Bow Island, Alberta

2 pounds ground beef
1 medium onion, chopped
2 cans (15 ounces *each*) Italian tomato sauce
1 can (16 ounces) kidney beans, rinsed and drained
1 can (14-1/2 ounces) stewed tomatoes
1 can (12 ounces) whole kernel corn, undrained
Shredded cheddar cheese
Tortilla chips

In a large saucepan, cook beef and onion over medium heat until the meat is no longer pink; drain. Add the tomato sauce, kidney beans, stewed tomatoes and corn; bring to a boil. Reduce heat; simmer, uncovered, for 10 minutes. Sprinkle with cheese. Serve with tortilla chips. **Yield: 10 servings (2-1/2 quarts).**

ZESTY CHEESE SOUP

My husband and I are retired, but we still look for shortcut recipes like this one that I received from a great-niece. You will likely have the majority of ingredients for this colorful soup in your pantry. To save even more time, I start warming the canned ingredients on the stovetop while I cube the cheese.

—Modie Phillips, Lubbock, Texas

1 can (15-1/4 ounces) whole kernel corn, drained
1 can (15 ounces) pinto beans, rinsed and drained
1 can (14-1/2 ounces) chicken broth
1 can (10 ounces) diced tomatoes and green chilies, undrained
1 can (10 ounces) premium chunk white chicken, drained
1 can (4 ounces) chopped green chilies
1 pound process American cheese (Velveeta), cubed
Crushed tortilla chips, optional

In a 3-qt. saucepan, combine the first seven ingredients. Cook and stir until cheese is melted. Garnish with tortilla chips if desired. **Yield: 6-8 servings (2 quarts).**

GREEN CHILI PORK STEW

GREEN CHILI PORK STEW

Anyone living in or visiting the Southwest knows green chilies are a staple. I grew up on this delicacy and thought everyone should know how mouth-watering it is. Serve it with a salad and freshly baked bread for a complete meal.

—Carrie Burton, Sierra Vista, Arizona

2-1/2 to 3 pounds boneless pork shoulder *or* butt, cut into 1-inch cubes
1 tablespoon canola oil
1 cup chopped onion
3 garlic cloves, minced
2 cups water
1 can (28 ounces) stewed tomatoes
1 to 2 cans (4 ounces *each*) chopped green chilies
2 cups cubed peeled potatoes
1 tablespoon chopped fresh cilantro
2 teaspoons ground cumin
2 teaspoons dried oregano
2 teaspoons fennel seed
1 teaspoon salt
1/4 teaspoon pepper
1 can (15 ounces) pinto beans, rinsed and drained

In a soup kettle or Dutch oven, brown pork in oil in over medium heat on all sides. Add onion and garlic; saute for 3-5 minutes. Drain. Add the water, tomatoes, chilies, potatoes and seasonings; bring to a boil. Reduce heat; cover and simmer for 45 minutes.

Add the pinto beans; cover and simmer for 20-30 minutes or until the meat and vegetables are tender. Ladle into bowls and serve. **Yield: 8-10 servings.**

SOPA DE TORTILLA

Remove to paper towels; pat dry. Drain, reserving 2 tablespoons oil in skillet. Add pasilla chilies; cook and stir for 1 minute or until lightly toasted. With a slotted spoon, remove to paper towels to drain.

In a large saucepan, saute onion and garlic in remaining oil until tender. Add tomato mixture; cook and stir over medium heat for 10 minutes or until very thick. Add the broth, corn, chicken and epazote; bring to a boil. Reduce heat; cover and simmer for 30 minutes. Stir in lime juice.

Ladle soup into bowls; top with tortilla strips. Sprinkle with pasilla chilies. Garnish with avocado and lime if desired. **Yield: 4-6 servings.**

TEXAS TURKEY SOUP

I'm not really fond of soup, so I was a little hesitant to try this recipe. But after some adjustments to suit my family's taste, I've come to love this one-of-a-kind delight.

—Betty Bakas, Lakehills, Texas

SOPA DE TORTILLA

Sopa de Tortilla, or Tortilla Soup, is a popular broth-based soup with flavor and texture in every spoonful. This traditional version created by our home economists blends tender chicken and corn with a light broth that gets its spark from onions, garlic, chilies and hot peppers.

Taste of Home Test Kitchen, Greendale, Wisconsin

1	can (14-1/2 ounces) diced tomatoes, drained
1	serrano pepper, seeded and chopped
1/2	cup plus 1 tablespoon canola oil, *divided*
6	corn tortillas (6 inches), halved and cut into 1/4-inch strips
2	dried pasilla chilies, stems removed, seeded and cut into 1/2-inch pieces
1/2	cup finely chopped onion
2	garlic cloves, minced
6	cups chicken broth
1-1/2	cups fresh *or* frozen corn, thawed
3/4	cup shredded cooked chicken
1	tablespoon minced fresh epazote *or* 1 teaspoon dried epazote
1	tablespoon lime juice

Cubed avocado and lime wedges, optional

In a blender, combine tomatoes and serrano pepper. Cover and process until smooth; set aside. In a large skillet, heat 1/2 cup oil over medium heat. Add tortilla strips; cook and stir until golden brown and crisp.

8	cups chicken broth
4	cups cubed cooked turkey
2	large white onions, halved
2	celery ribs, sliced
3	medium carrots, sliced
1	cup *each* frozen corn, cut green beans and peas
2	bay leaves
1/2	to 1 teaspoon dried tarragon
3/4	teaspoon garlic powder
1/4	to 1/2 teaspoon hot pepper sauce

Salt and pepper to taste

1-1/2	cups uncooked noodles
1	tablespoon cornstarch
1	tablespoon water

In a Dutch oven or soup kettle, combine the chicken broth, turkey, vegetables, seasonings, hot pepper sauce and salt and pepper. Bring to a boil. Reduce heat; cover and simmer for 20-30 minutes or until vegetables are tender.

Return to a boil; add noodles. Reduce heat; cover and simmer for 15-20 minutes or until noodles are tender.

Combine cornstarch and water until smooth; add to soup. Bring to a boil; boil for 2 minutes, stirring constantly. Remove bay leaves. **Yield: 10-12 servings (3 quarts).**

FOUR-STAR CHILI

This spicy chili features traditional ingredients like ground beef, green peppers and tomatoes, but carrots and white beans make it deliciously different. Serve it over rice for a hearty meal.
—Frank Fenti, Hornell, New York

1-1/2   pounds ground beef
   2   large green peppers, diced
   1   medium onion, diced
   4   garlic cloves, minced
   1   can (28 ounces) crushed tomatoes
   1   can (15-1/2 ounces) great northern beans, rinsed and drained
   1   can (14-1/2 ounces) chicken broth
   1   medium carrot, chopped
   1   celery rib, chopped
   2   jalapeno peppers, finely chopped
2-1/2   teaspoons pepper blend
   1   teaspoon paprika
  1/2   teaspoon crushed red pepper flakes
Hot cooked rice
Sour cream
Shredded Colby cheese

In a soup kettle or Dutch oven, cook the beef, green peppers, onion and garlic over medium heat until meat is no longer pink; drain. Add the tomatoes, beans, broth, carrot, celery, jalapenos and seasonings; bring to a boil.

Reduce heat; cover and simmer for 1-1/2 hours or until thick and bubbly. Serve with rice, sour cream and cheese. **Yield: 18 servings (4-1/4 quarts).**

Editor's Note: When cutting hot peppers, disposable gloves are recommended. Avoid touching your face.

FOUR-STAR CHILI

SOUTHWEST BARLEY STEW

SOUTHWEST BARLEY STEW

You won't miss the meat in this comforting medley of tender barley, tomatoes, lentils and green chilies. The not-too-spicy flavor will quickly make it a favorite.
—Mary Sullivan, Spokane, Washington

  1   cup chopped onion
  1   cup chopped celery
  1   garlic clove, minced
  3   tablespoons canola oil
  2   quarts beef *or* chicken broth
  2   cans (14-1/2 ounces *each*) diced tomatoes, undrained
  1   cup medium pearl barley
  1   cup lentils
  1   can (4 ounces) chopped green chilies
  1   tablespoon chili powder
  2   teaspoons ground cumin
  1   teaspoon ground coriander
1/8   teaspoon cayenne pepper

In a soup kettle or Dutch oven, saute onion, celery and garlic in oil until tender. Add the remaining ingredients. Bring to a boil. Reduce heat; cover and simmer for 1 hour or until the barley is tender, stirring occasionally. **Yield: 12 servings (3 quarts).**

Easy Kitchen Tips

When used in soups and stews, barley and beans absorb a lot of the broth. If you like barley and beans in your soup but the leftovers are too thick, just add extra chicken, beef or vegetable broth to the leftovers while reheating to achieve the desired consistency.

SPICY STEAK STEW

SPICY STEAK STEW

One night, I was running late and didn't know what to make for dinner. So I tossed some steak and everything else I could think of into the pressure cooker. It was a great last-minute meal that tasted very good.

—Wendy Hughes, Easton, Pennsylvania

- 2 cups cubed beef flank steak (1/2-inch cubes)
- 1 medium onion, sliced
- 1 garlic clove, minced
- 1 tablespoon canola oil
- 1 can (14 ounces) onion-seasoned *or* regular beef broth
- 1 can (14-1/2 ounces) Italian stewed tomatoes
- 2 cups diced peeled potato
- 1 cup coarsely chopped fresh broccoli
- 1 celery rib, thinly sliced
- 1/2 cup minced fresh parsley
- 2 teaspoons Worcestershire sauce
- 1/4 teaspoon *each* salt, pepper and crushed red pepper flakes
- 1 tablespoon cornstarch
- 1 tablespoon cold water

In a pressure cooker, brown steak, onion and garlic in oil until meat is no longer pink; drain. Add broth; simmer for 10 minutes. Add the vegetables, parsley, Worcestershire sauce and seasonings.

Close cover securely; place pressure regulator on vent pipe. Bring cooker to full pressure over high heat. Reduce heat to medium-high and cook for 15 minutes. (Pressure regulator should maintain a slow steady rocking motion;

adjust heat if needed.) Immediately cool according to manufacturer's directions until pressure is completely reduced.

In a small bowl, combine cornstarch and water until smooth; stir into stew. Bring to a boil over medium heat; cook for 2 minutes or until thickened. **Yield: 6 servings.**

BLACK BEAN GAZPACHO

I first tried this colorful, chilled soup at my best friend's house during one of the hottest summers I can remember. The healthy, garden-fresh combination really hit the spot!

—Shelley Graff, Philo, Illinois

- 3 cans (11-1/2 ounces *each*) picante V8 juice
- 4 medium tomatoes, seeded and chopped
- 1 can (15 ounces) black beans, rinsed and drained
- 1 cup cubed fully cooked ham
- 1/2 cup *each* chopped green, sweet yellow and red pepper
- 1/2 cup chopped cucumber
- 1/2 cup chopped zucchini
- 1/4 cup finely chopped green onions
- 2 tablespoons Italian salad dressing
- 3/4 teaspoon salt
- 1/8 to 1/4 teaspoon hot pepper sauce

Combine all of the ingredients in a large bowl. Cover and refrigerate for at least 2 hours. **Yield: 10 servings.**

BLACK BEAN GAZPACHO

CHICKEN CHILI

Loaded with hearty beans and tender chicken, this zippy chili really warms us up on chilly winter nights.

—Lisa Goodman, Bloomington, Minnesota

4-1/2 cups low-sodium chicken broth
2 cans (15 ounces *each*) black beans, rinsed and drained
1/2 cup *each* chopped green, yellow and sweet red pepper
1/4 cup chopped onion
1 tablespoon chili powder
1-1/2 teaspoons paprika
1 to 1-1/2 teaspoons pepper
1 to 1-1/2 teaspoons crushed red pepper flakes
1 to 1-1/2 teaspoons ground cumin
1/2 teaspoon salt-free seasoning blend
Dash cayenne pepper
2 cups cubed cooked chicken breast

In a 3-qt. saucepan, bring broth to a boil. Reduce heat; add the beans, peppers, onion and seasonings. Cover and simmer 15 minutes. Add chicken; simmer for 30 minutes. **Yield: 7 servings.**

SALSA CHICKEN SOUP

You wouldn't guess that this quick-and-easy soup is low in fat. I sometimes use medium or hot salsa in this recipe for extra zip.

—Becky Christman, Bridgeton, Missouri

1/2 pound boneless skinless chicken breasts, cubed
1 can (14-1/2 ounces) chicken broth
1-3/4 cups water
1 to 2 teaspoons chili powder
1 cup frozen corn
1 cup salsa
Shredded Monterey Jack cheese *or* pepper Jack cheese, optional

In a large saucepan, combine chicken, broth, water and chili powder. Bring to a boil. Reduce heat; cover and simmer for 5 minutes. Add corn; return to a boil.

Reduce heat; simmer, uncovered, for 5 minutes or until chicken is no longer pink and corn is tender. Add salsa and heat through. Garnish with cheese if desired. **Yield: 6 servings.**

MEXICAN CHICKEN CORN CHOWDER

MEXICAN CHICKEN CORN CHOWDER

I like to make this smooth, creamy soup when company comes to visit. Its robust flavor is full of Southwestern flair. My family enjoys dipping thick slices of homemade bread in this chowder to soak up every mouth-watering bite.

—Susan Garoutte, Georgetown, Texas

1-1/2 pounds boneless skinless chicken breasts, cut into 1-inch pieces
1/2 cup chopped onion
1 to 2 garlic cloves, minced
3 tablespoons butter
1 cup hot water
2 teaspoons chicken bouillon granules
1/2 to 1 teaspoon ground cumin
2 cups half-and-half cream
2 cups (8 ounces) shredded Monterey Jack cheese
1 can (14-3/4 ounces) cream-style corn
1 can (4 ounces) chopped green chilies, undrained
1/4 to 1 teaspoon hot pepper sauce
1 medium tomato, chopped
Minced fresh cilantro, optional

In a Dutch oven, brown chicken, onion and garlic in butter until chicken is no longer pink. Add the water, bouillon and cumin; bring to a boil. Reduce heat; cover and simmer for 5 minutes.

Stir in the cream, cheese, corn, chilies and hot pepper sauce. Cook and stir over low heat until the cheese is melted; add tomato. Sprinkle with cilantro if desired. **Yield: 6-8 servings (2 quarts).**

TORTILLA SOUP

TORTILLA SOUP

Corn tortillas provide this soup with scrumptious texture. It's a fast-growing favorite with my family and friends. I especially like this recipe because it can be made quickly and easily, and it can be served as an appetizer or main dish.

—Pat Cox, Bogata, Texas

- 1   medium tomato, quartered
- 1   can (14-1/2 ounces) whole peeled tomatoes with liquid
- 1   small onion, quartered
- 1   garlic clove
- 2   cans (10-1/2 ounces *each*) condensed chicken broth, undiluted
- 1/2   teaspoon chili powder
- 1/2   teaspoon salt
- 1/4   teaspoon pepper
- 1/4   teaspoon ground coriander
- 1/4   teaspoon ground cumin
- 1   tablespoon minced fresh cilantro
- 6   corn tortillas (6 inches)
- 1/4   cup canola oil

Sour cream

Shredded cheddar *or* Monterey Jack cheese

Place the tomatoes, onion and garlic in a blender; cover and process until smooth. Transfer to a large saucepan. Add chicken broth and seasonings. Bring to a boil. Reduce heat; simmer, uncovered, for 3 minutes.

Meanwhile, cut tortillas into 1/4-in. strips; fry in hot oil until crisp and brown. Drain on paper towels. Ladle soup into bowls; top with tortilla strips, sour cream and cheese. **Yield: 4 servings.**

SOUTHWESTERN MEAT AND POTATO STEW

Even before it got cold outside last fall, my husband asked me to make this stew twice. In fact, here at home, our name for this meat and potato medley is "Tom's Favorite Stew."

—Linda Schwarz, Bertrand, Nebraska

- 2   pounds ground beef
- 1   large onion, chopped
- 1   cup water, *divided*
- 1   can (28 ounces) diced tomatoes, undrained
- 1   package (16 ounces) frozen corn
- 3   medium potatoes, peeled and cubed
- 1   cup salsa
- 1   teaspoon salt, optional
- 1   teaspoon ground cumin
- 1/2   teaspoon garlic powder
- 1/2   teaspoon pepper
- 2   tablespoons all-purpose flour

In a Dutch oven or large kettle, cook beef and onion over medium heat until meat is no longer pink; drain. Add 3/4 cup water, vegetables, salsa, salt if desired, cumin, garlic powder and pepper. Bring to a boil; reduce heat. Cover and simmer for 1-1/2 hours.

Combine flour and remaining water until smooth; gradually stir into stew. Bring to a boil; cook and stir for 2 minutes or until thickened. **Yield: 6 servings.**

SOUTHWESTERN MEAT AND POTATO STEW

ZIPPY CHICKEN CORN CHOWDER

ZIPPY CHICKEN CORN CHOWDER

In this full-bodied chowder, corn is complemented by a zesty pepper flavor that you can adjust to suit your family's palate. Serve it with warm, fresh-from-the-oven rolls and a crisp salad for a completely satisfying meal.

—Doris Krise, Edwardsburg, Michigan

  2   pounds boneless skinless chicken breasts, cubed
  4   tablespoons butter, *divided*
  1   large sweet red pepper, chopped
  2   medium leeks, chopped
  3   tablespoons all-purpose flour
  1   tablespoon paprika
  4   cups chicken broth
  2   medium potatoes, cubed
  4   cups frozen corn
  1   tablespoon Worcestershire sauce
  1   teaspoon salt
1/2   to 1 teaspoon hot pepper sauce
  1   cup half-and-half cream

In a soup kettle or Dutch oven, saute cubed chicken breast in 2 tablespoons butter until lightly browned. Remove from pan, set aside and keep warm.

In the same pan, saute the red pepper in remaining butter until tender. Add the chopped leeks; cook for 1 minute. Stir in the flour and paprika until blended. Gradually stir in the chicken broth. Add the potatoes; bring to a boil. Reduce heat; cover and simmer for 15 minutes or until the potatoes are tender.

Stir in the corn, Worcestershire sauce, salt, hot pepper sauce and reserved chicken; bring to a boil. Reduce heat.

Cook, uncovered, for 5-8 minutes or until corn is tender, stirring occasionally. Stir in cream and heat through (do not boil). **Yield: 10 servings (2-1/2 quarts).**

STUFFED ROAST PEPPER SOUP

After sampling a similar soup at a summer resort, my daughter and I invented this tough-to-beat version. Using a colorful variety of peppers gives it plenty of eye appeal.

—Betty Vig, Viroqua, Wisconsin

  2   pounds ground beef
1/2   medium onion, chopped
  6   cups water
  8   beef bouillon cubes
  2   cans (28 ounces *each*) diced tomatoes, undrained
  2   cups cooked rice
  2   teaspoon salt
1/2   teaspoon pepper
1/2   teaspoon paprika
  3   green, sweet yellow *or* red peppers, seeded and chopped

In a large Dutch oven or soup kettle, cook ground beef with onion until the meat is brown and the onion is tender; drain. Add water, bouillon cubes, tomatoes, rice and seasonings.

Bring to a boil; reduce heat and simmer, covered, for 1 hour. Add peppers; cook, uncovered, for 10-15 minutes or just until tender. **Yield: 14-16 servings (4 quarts).**

STUFFED ROAST PEPPER SOUP

Sides & Salads

SOUTHWEST PORK AND BEAN SALAD, P. 50

BEEF FAJITA SALAD

BEEF FAJITA SALAD

This easy-to-assemble salad features colorful peppers, beans, tomato and tender strips of beef. Although the beef marinates for only 10 minutes, it gets great flavor from the lime juice, cilantro and chili powder.

—Ardeena Harris, Roanoke, Alabama

1/4	cup lime juice
2	tablespoons minced fresh cilantro
1	garlic clove, minced
1	teaspoon chili powder
3/4	pound boneless beef sirloin steak, cut into thin strips
1	medium green pepper, julienned
1	medium sweet red pepper, julienned
1	medium onion, sliced and halved
1	teaspoon olive oil
1	can (16 ounces) kidney beans, rinsed and drained
4	cups torn mixed salad greens
1	medium tomato, chopped
4	tablespoons sour cream
2	tablespoons salsa

In a large resealable plastic bag, combine the lime juice, cilantro, garlic and chili powder; add beef. Seal bag and turn to coat; refrigerate for 10 minutes, turning once.

Meanwhile, in a nonstick skillet, cook the peppers and onion in oil over medium-high heat for 5 minutes or until tender. Remove and keep warm. Add beef with marinade to the skillet; cook and stir for 4-5 minutes or until meat

is tender and mixture comes to a boil. Add beans and pepper mixture; heat through.

Divide the salad greens and tomato among four bowls; top each with 1-1/4 cups beef mixture, 1 tablespoon sour cream and 1-1/2 teaspoons salsa. **Yield: 4 servings.**

CALIFORNIA-STYLE SPANISH RICE

Back in the 1920s, my great-aunt Mable lived with her four children in an old World War I army tent. She had to be creative in her cooking, and this was one dish she relied on frequently.

—Renee Randall, Port Richey, Florida

4	bacon strips, diced
3/4	cup chopped onion
2	tablespoons olive oil
1	cup uncooked long grain rice
1	can (14-1/2 ounces) beef broth
1	cup diced green pepper
1	cup diced sweet red pepper
1	can (14-1/2 ounces) stewed tomatoes

In a large skillet, cook bacon until crisp; remove to paper towels. Drain, reserving 2 tablespoons drippings. In the drippings, saute onion until tender. Remove and set aside.

In a small skillet, heat oil over medium heat. Add rice; cook and stir until golden brown. Reduce heat; stir in broth. Cover and simmer for 20 minutes. Stir in the bacon, onion, peppers and tomatoes. Cover and simmer 25-30 minutes longer or until rice is tender and most of the liquid is absorbed. **Yield: 8-10 servings.**

CALIFORNIA-STYLE SPANISH RICE

CHEESY CORN SPOON BREAD

CHEESY CORN SPOON BREAD

Homey and comforting, this custard-like side dish is a much-requested recipe at potlucks and holiday dinners. The jalapeno pepper adds just the right "bite." Seconds helpings of this tasty casserole are common...leftovers are not.

—Katherine Franklin, Carbondale, Illinois

1	medium onion, chopped
1/4	cup butter, cubed
2	eggs
2	cups (16 ounces) sour cream
1	can (15-1/4 ounces) whole kernel corn, drained
1	can (14-3/4 ounces) cream-style corn
1/4	teaspoon salt
1/4	teaspoon pepper
1	package (8-1/2 ounces) corn bread/muffin mix
1	medium jalapeno pepper, minced
2	cups (8 ounces) shredded cheddar cheese, *divided*

In a large skillet, saute the onion in butter until tender; set onion aside.

In a large bowl, beat the eggs; add sour cream, both cans of corn, salt and pepper. Stir in the corn bread mix just until blended. Fold in the sauteed onion, jalapeno and 1-1/2 cups of cheddar cheese.

Transfer to a greased shallow 3-qt. baking dish. Sprinkle with the remaining cheese. Bake, uncovered, at 375° for 35-40 minutes or until a toothpick inserted near the center comes out clean; cool slightly. **Yield: 12-15 servings.**

***Editor's Note:** When cutting hot peppers, disposable gloves are recommended. Avoid touching your face.*

FIESTA SIDE SALAD

You will want to make extra of this colorful side because the flavors only get better the second day. Toasting whole cumin seeds and then grinding them adds extra flavor to the salad. If you don't have whole cumin seeds, substitute 1/4 teaspoon of ground cumin—but don't toast it.

—Michelle Chicoine, Missoula, Montana

2/3	cup uncooked long grain rice
2	cups frozen corn, thawed
1	can (15 ounces) black beans, rinsed and drained
6	green onions, sliced
1/4	cup pickled jalapeno slices, chopped
1/4	cup canola oil
2	tablespoons cider vinegar
1	tablespoon lime juice
1	teaspoon chili powder
1	teaspoon molasses
1/2	teaspoon salt
1/2	teaspoon cumin seeds, toasted and ground

Cook rice according to package directions. Meanwhile, in a large bowl, combine the corn, beans, onions and jalapenos. In a jar with a tight-fitting lid, combine the remaining ingredients; shake well.

Stir rice into corn mixture. Add dressing and toss to coat. Cover salad and refrigerate for at least 2 hours. **Yield: 8 servings.**

FIESTA SIDE SALAD

ENSALADA DE NOPALITOS

ENSALADA DE NOPALITOS

Also known as Cactus Salad, Ensalada de Nopalitos is a traditional Southwestern dish. Nopalitos, or cactus pads, are available in cans or jars as well as fresh. If you wish, you may substitute green beans for the cactus.

—Taste of Home Test Kitchen, Greendale, Wisconsin

- 1 jar (15 ounces) sliced cactus, rinsed and drained
- 2 medium tomatoes, cut into 1-inch pieces
- 1/4 cup finely chopped onion
- 2 tablespoons chopped fresh cilantro
- 3 tablespoons canola oil
- 1 tablespoon rice vinegar
- 1 teaspoon lime juice
- 1 teaspoon dried Mexican oregano
- 1/8 teaspoon salt
- 1/4 cup crumbled queso fresco

In a large bowl, combine the cactus, tomatoes, onion and cilantro. In a jar with a tight-fitting lid, combine the oil, vinegar, lime juice, oregano and salt; shake well. Just before serving, drizzle over salad and toss to coat. Sprinkle with queso fresco. **Yield: 4 servings.**

SOUTHWESTERN CHICKEN SALAD

We have five children who love salads, chicken and Mexican food. So, I combined all three to make this satisfying main dish salad. There is no groaning from anyone when I set the crunchy, pleasing combination on the table!

—Margaret Yost, Casstown, Ohio

- 1/3 cup Thousand Island salad dressing
- 1/3 cup salsa
- 1/4 cup sour cream
- 1 teaspoon seasoned salt
- 1 teaspoon garlic powder
- 1/2 teaspoon salt-free lemon-pepper seasoning
- 1/4 teaspoon cayenne pepper
- 1 pound boneless skinless chicken breasts, cut into 1/4-inch strips
- 1 tablespoon olive oil
- 1 medium sweet red pepper, cut into 1/4-inch strips
- 1 medium green pepper, cut into 1/4-inch strips
- 2 teaspoons lime juice
- 12 cups torn romaine
- 1-1/2 cups (6 ounces) shredded cheddar cheese
- 1 cup shredded red cabbage
- 1 medium tomato, chopped
- 1 medium carrot, grated

Tortilla chips

In a small bowl, combine the salad dressing, salsa and sour cream. Cover and refrigerate until serving.

Combine the seasonings; sprinkle over chicken. In a nonstick skillet, brown chicken in oil for 3 minutes on each side. Add peppers; saute 2-3 minutes longer or until chicken juices run clear. Drizzle chicken and peppers with lime juice; keep warm.

In a large bowl, toss the romaine, cheese, cabbage, tomato and carrot. Add chicken mixture. Serve over chips; drizzle with dressing. **Yield: 8 servings.**

SOUTHWESTERN CHICKEN SALAD

SALSA PASTA 'N' BEANS

SALSA PASTA 'N' BEANS

SALSA PASTA 'N' BEANS

This warm side dish is well-seasoned with cumin, cilantro and salsa, so it adds a little pep to dinnertime. For people who like even more spice, it is easy to substitute mild salsa with a medium or hot variety.

—Laura Perry, Chester Springs, Pennsylvania

8	ounces uncooked bow tie pasta
1/2	cup chopped onion
1	medium sweet yellow pepper, chopped
1	tablespoon olive oil
2	teaspoons minced garlic
1	can (16 ounces) red beans, rinsed and drained
3/4	cup vegetable broth
3/4	cup salsa
2	teaspoons ground cumin
1/3	cup minced fresh cilantro

Cook pasta according to package directions. Meanwhile, in a large skillet, saute onion and yellow pepper in oil for 3-4 minutes or until crisp-tender. Add garlic; cook 1-2 minutes longer or until tender.

Stir in the beans, broth, salsa and cumin. Bring to a boil. Reduce heat; simmer, uncovered, for 5-6 minutes or until heated through. Drain pasta; stir into bean mixture. Sprinkle with cilantro. **Yield: 4 servings.**

Easy Kitchen Tips

With its slightly sharp flavor, cilantro—also known as Chinese parsley—gives a distinctive taste to Mexican, Latin American and Asian dishes. Like all other fresh herbs, cilantro should be used as soon as possible.

SOUTHWESTERN BARLEY SALAD

The fresh flavor of cilantro really comes through in this colorful side that's zesty but not too hot. It also makes a great light dinner entree when served with sesame breadsticks and sherbet or sugar cookies for dessert.

—Tommi Roylance, Charlo, Montana

3	cups cooked medium pearl barley
1	can (15 ounces) black beans, rinsed and drained
1-1/2	cups frozen corn, thawed
1-1/2	cups diced seeded tomatoes
1	cup frozen peas, thawed
1/4	cup minced fresh cilantro
1	teaspoon salt
1/4	teaspoon pepper
1/2	cup water
3	tablespoons lemon juice
1	tablespoon finely chopped onion
1	tablespoon canola oil
2	garlic cloves, minced
8	lettuce leaves
1	ripe avocado, peeled and sliced
2	medium tomatoes, cut into wedges

In a bowl, combine the first eight ingredients. In a jar with a tight-fitting lid, combine the water, lemon juice, onion, oil and garlic; shake well. Pour over barley mixture and toss to coat. Serve on lettuce-lined plates. Garnish with avocado and tomatoes. **Yield: 8 servings.**

SOUTHWESTERN BARLEY SALAD

PEPPER JACK POTATOES

I make these nicely seasoned potatoes all the time because they seem to go with anything. At an economical price per serving, this cheesy accompaniment is sure to satisfy several guests without straining your budget.

—Barbara Nowakowski, North Tonawanda, New York

6	medium potatoes, peeled and cut into 1/4-inch slices
1	medium onion, sliced
1/3	cup butter, melted
1/2	teaspoon salt
1/4	teaspoon chili powder
1/8	teaspoon cayenne pepper
1/8	teaspoon pepper
2-1/2	cups (10 ounces) shredded pepper Jack *or* Monterey Jack cheese, *divided*

Salsa, optional

In a large bowl, combine potatoes and onion. Combine the butter and seasonings; drizzle over the potato mixture; toss to coat. Place half in a greased 13-in. x 9-in. baking dish. Sprinkle with half of the cheese; top with remaining potato mixture.

Cover and bake at 400° for 45-50 minutes or until potatoes are tender. Uncover; sprinkle with remaining cheese. Bake 5 minutes longer or until cheese is melted. Serve with salsa if desired. **Yield: 10 servings.**

SALSA CORN CAKES

This recipe is super with fresh or canned corn. I whip up these patties to serve alongside nachos or tacos on hot summer evenings. The salsa is subtle but packs in a punch.

—Lisa Boettcher, Rosebush, Michigan

2	packages (3 ounces *each*) cream cheese, softened
1/4	cup butter, melted
6	eggs
1	cup milk
1-1/2	cups all-purpose flour
1/2	cup cornmeal
1	teaspoon baking powder
1	teaspoon salt
1	can (15-1/4 ounces) whole kernel corn, drained
1/2	cup salsa, drained

SALSA CORN CAKES

1/4	cup minced green onions

Sour cream and additional salsa

In a large bowl, beat cream cheese and butter until smooth; add the eggs and mix well. Beat in the milk until smooth. Combine the flour, cornmeal, baking powder and salt just until moistened. Fold in the corn, salsa and green onions.

Pour batter by 1/4 cupfuls onto a greased hot griddle. Turn when bubbles form on top; cook until the second side is golden brown. Serve with sour cream and salsa. **Yield: 6-8 servings.**

EGGPLANT MEXICANO

Salsa jazzes up eggplant slices in this speedy dish. We had an overabundance of eggplant some years ago, which made this recipe catch my eye. My husband and I think it's delicious.

—Alyce De Roos, Corunna, Ontario

1/2	cup canola oil
1	teaspoon garlic powder
1	teaspoon dried oregano
1	medium eggplant, peeled and cut into 1/2-inch slices
2/3	cup salsa, warmed
1/2	cup shredded Monterey Jack cheese

In a small bowl, combine the oil, garlic powder and oregano; brush over both sides of eggplant. Grill, uncovered, over medium heat for 4 minutes on each side or until tender. Spoon a small amount of salsa into the center of each; sprinkle with cheese. **Yield: 6 servings.**

RANCH BEANS

RANCH BEANS

This sweet and tangy side dish uses lots of convenient canned goods, so it's a snap to throw together. The recipe, given to me by a friend, makes a lovely addition to a picnic.
—Barbara Gordon, Roswell, Georgia

  1   can (16 ounces) kidney beans, rinsed and drained
  1   can (15-3/4 ounces) pork and beans, undrained
  1   can (15 ounces) lima beans, rinsed and drained
  1   can (14-1/2 ounces) cut green beans, drained
  1   bottle (12 ounces) chili sauce
3/4 cup packed brown sugar
  1   small onion, chopped

In a 3-qt. slow cooker, combine all ingredients. Cover and cook on high for 3-4 hours or until heated through. **Yield: 8-10 servings.**

CHILI-CHEESE MASHED POTATOES

Instant mashed potatoes with garlic, green chilies and cheese jazz up this speedy side. People can't get enough!
—Peter Halferty, Corpus Christi, Texas

2-3/4 cups water
   1   cup milk
1-1/2 teaspoons salt
   1   tablespoon butter
   3   garlic cloves, minced
   3   cups instant mashed potato flakes

  2   cans (4 ounces *each*) chopped green chilies
  1   cup (4 ounces) shredded Mexican cheese blend

In a large saucepan, bring the water, milk and salt to a boil. Add the butter, garlic, potato flakes and chilies; stir until thickened. Sprinkle with cheese. **Yield: 6 servings.**

PEPPERED CILANTRO RICE

This colorful confetti rice is a traditional dish in Puerto Rico. We enjoy it in the summer alongside grilled shrimp kabobs, but it is delicious with most any entree.
—Laura Perry, Chester Springs, Pennsylvania

  1   small onion, finely chopped
  1   small sweet yellow pepper, finely chopped
  1   small sweet red pepper, finely chopped
  2   garlic cloves, minced
  1   tablespoon olive oil
  2   cups water
  1   cup uncooked long grain rice
3/4 teaspoon salt
1/4 teaspoon pepper
  2   tablespoons minced fresh cilantro

In a large saucepan, saute the onion, peppers and garlic in oil until crisp-tender. Add the water, rice, salt and pepper. Bring to a boil. Reduce heat; cover and simmer for 18-22 minutes or until rice is tender.

Remove from the heat; fluff with a fork. Stir in cilantro. **Yield: 6 servings.**

PEPPERED CILANTRO RICE

SPICY CREAMED CORN

SPICY CREAMED CORN

One of my family's favorite vegetables is corn, and this quick dish is so simple to prepare. It tastes extraordinary and goes very well with turkey and chicken. It's a no-fuss way to add a touch of spice and homemade goodness to your meal.

—Nancy McDonald, Burns, Wyoming

- 1 package (3 ounces) cream cheese, cubed
- 1 can (15-1/4 ounces) whole kernel corn, drained
- 1 can (4 ounces) chopped green chilies
- 1/4 cup sliced green onions
- 1/4 cup chopped sweet red pepper

In a large saucepan, combine all the ingredients. Cook over medium heat until cream cheese is melted and mixture is blended, stirring often. **Yield: 4 servings.**

RED BEANS 'N' BROWN RICE

Here's a flavorful twist on traditional red beans and rice. The sweetness of the molasses and ketchup contrasts nicely with the bold garlic and onion. Some people comment that the taste reminds them of barbecued beans.

—Rita Farmer, Greendale, Wisconsin

- 1/2 cup chopped onion
- 2 garlic cloves, minced
- 2 teaspoons canola oil
- 2 cans (15-1/2 ounces *each*) red beans, rinsed and drained
- 1 can (4 ounces) chopped green chilies
- 1/2 cup light beer *or* beef broth
- 1/4 cup ketchup *or* seafood cocktail sauce
- 1/4 cup molasses

- 1 tablespoon chili powder
- 1 tablespoon cider vinegar
- 2 teaspoons reduced-sodium soy sauce
- 3 cups hot cooked brown *or* white rice

In a large saucepan, saute onion and garlic in oil until tender. Add the beans, chilies, beer, ketchup, molasses, chili powder, vinegar and soy sauce. Bring to a boil. Reduce heat; simmer, uncovered, for 20-30 minutes. Serve with rice. **Yield: 4 servings.**

SOUTHWESTERN SALAD

You get an explosion of Southwestern flavor in every bite of this deliciously different salad. I have found that it is a favorite of kids of all ages because it combines beans, cheese, fresh vegetables and crunchy corn chips.

—Jerri Moror, Rio Rancho, New Mexico

- 2-1/2 cups corn chips
- 1/2 head iceberg lettuce, torn
- 1 cup (4 ounces) shredded Mexican cheese blend *or* cheddar cheese
- 1 can (15 ounces) pinto beans, rinsed and drained
- 1 small tomato, seeded and diced
- 1/4 to 1/2 cup salad dressing of your choice
- 2 tablespoons sliced green onions
- 1 to 2 tablespoons chopped green chilies
- 1 small avocado, peeled and sliced

In a serving bowl or platter, toss together the chips, lettuce, cheese, beans, tomato, salad dressing, onions and green chilies. Top with avocado. Serve salad immediately. **Yield: 8 servings.**

SOUTHWESTERN SALAD

CORN BREAD SALAD

CORN BREAD SALAD

Despite my sometimes hectic schedule, I enjoy cooking for family and friends. This recipe is one of my favorites.
—Pam Holloway, Marion, Louisiana

- 1 package (8-1/2 ounces) corn bread/muffin mix
- 2 cans (11 ounces *each*) Mexicorn, drained, *divided*
- 3 medium tomatoes, diced
- 3/4 cup chopped green pepper
- 1 medium onion, chopped
- 1 cup mayonnaise
- 4 bacon strips, cooked and crumbled

Prepare corn bread batter according to the package directions; stir in one can of Mexicorn. Bake according to package directions. Cool and crumble.

In a large bowl, combine the crumbled corn bread, tomatoes, green pepper, onion and remaining can of corn. Add mayonnaise; toss to coat. Sprinkle with bacon. Serve or refrigerate. **Yield: 10-12 servings.**

FRIJOLES Y CHORIZO

Chorizo is a popular pork sausage that originated in Spain. Here, in this tasty and authentic side dish, our home economists slowly cook the flavorful meat before crumbling it into a zippy mixture of beans, peppers and seasonings.
—Taste of Home Test Kitchen, Greendale, Wisconsin

- 2 cups (1 pound) dried pinto beans
- 2 poblano peppers
- 2 serrano peppers
- 6 cups water
- 1 bay leaf
- 1/2 pound uncooked chorizo, casing removed
- 2 tablespoons lard
- 1 cup chopped onion
- 2 teaspoons salt
- 1/4 cup chopped fresh cilantro

Sort beans and rinse with cold water. Place beans in a Dutch oven; add water to cover by 2 in. Bring to a boil; boil for 2 minutes. Remove from heat; cover and let stand for 1 hour.

Place peppers on a baking sheet; broil 4 in. from the heat until skins blister, about 4 minutes. With tongs, rotate peppers a quarter turn. Broil and rotate until all sides are blistered and blackened. Immediately place peppers in a bowl; cover and let stand for 15 minutes. Peel off and discard charred skin. Remove stems and seeds. Chop peppers and set aside.

Drain and rinse pinto beans, discarding liquid. Return beans to the Dutch oven. Add 6 cups water and bay leaf; bring to a boil. Reduce heat; simmer, uncovered, for 1-1/2 to 2 hours or until beans are tender.

Meanwhile, crumble chorizo into a skillet; cook over medium heat for 6-8 minutes or until fully cooked. Drain and set aside. In the same skillet, melt lard. Add onion and reserved peppers; cook and stir until tender, about 5 minutes. Add the chorizo, pepper mixture and salt to the pinto beans. Simmer, uncovered, for 30 minutes. Discard bay leaf. Just before serving, stir in cilantro. **Yield: 16 servings (2 quarts).**

Editor's Note: When cutting hot peppers, disposable gloves are recommended. Avoid touching your face.

FRIJOLES Y CHORIZO

CANTINA PINTO BEANS

Cumin, cilantro and red pepper flakes lend a Southwestern flair to tender pinto beans in this recipe. This dish was inspired by one served at a Dallas, Texas restaurant. The chef added chunks of ham, but my version is meatless. It makes a great Tex-Mex side or a filling lunch when served with corn bread.

—Mrs. L.R. Larson, Sioux Falls, South Dakota

 2 cups (1 pound) dried pinto beans
 2 cans (14-1/2 ounces *each*) reduced-sodium chicken broth
 2 celery ribs, diced
 1/4 cup diced onion
 1/4 cup diced green pepper
 1 teaspoon ground cumin
 1/2 teaspoon rubbed sage
 1/4 teaspoon crushed red pepper flakes
 2 bay leaves
 1 garlic clove, minced
 2 cans (14-1/2 ounces *each*) Mexican diced tomatoes
 1/2 teaspoon salt
Minced fresh parsley

Sort beans and rinse with cold water. Place beans in a Dutch oven or soup kettle; add water to cover by 2 in. Bring to a boil; boil for 2 minutes. Remove from the heat; cover and let stand for 1 hour.

Drain and rinse beans, discarding liquid. Return beans to Dutch oven. Stir in the broth, celery, onion, green pepper, cumin, sage, pepper flakes, bay leaves and garlic. Bring to a boil. Reduce heat; simmer, uncovered, for 1 hour or until beans are very tender.

Discard bay leaves. Stir in tomatoes and salt. Simmer, uncovered, for 30 minutes or until heated through. Sprinkle with cilantro. **Yield: 10 servings.**

Easy Kitchen Tips

Many Southwestern recipes call for dried beans, but it can take a long time to cook them. To speed up the process, try this time-saving tip.

Prepare an entire bag of beans at once by soaking them overnight and cooking them in a large pot the next day.

Once the beans have been drained and cooled, place cupfuls in freezer bags and keep them in the freezer to use whenever a recipe calls for them.

BLACK-EYED PEAS 'N' PASTA

BLACK-EYED PEAS 'N' PASTA

Tradition has it that if you eat black-eyed peas on New Year's Day, you will enjoy prosperity throughout the upcoming year, but I like to serve this fun combination of bow tie pasta, peas and a tangy tomato sauce any time.

—Marie Malsch, Bridgman, Michigan

 1 cup chopped green pepper
 1/2 cup chopped onion
 1 jalapeno pepper, seeded and chopped
 3 garlic cloves, minced
 1 tablespoon olive oil
 1 can (28 ounces) crushed tomatoes
 1 can (15-1/2 ounces) black-eyed peas, rinsed and drained
 1 to 3 tablespoons minced fresh cilantro
 1 teaspoon cider vinegar
 1 teaspoon sugar
 1 teaspoon salt
 1/8 teaspoon pepper
 5 cups hot cooked bow tie pasta

In a large skillet, saute the green pepper, onion, jalapeno and garlic in oil for 5 minutes or until tender. Add tomatoes; bring to a boil. Simmer, uncovered, for 10 minutes. Stir in the peas, cilantro, vinegar, sugar, salt and pepper; simmer 10 minutes longer. Toss with pasta. **Yield: 6 servings.**

Editor's Note: When cutting hot peppers, disposable gloves are recommended. Avoid touching your face.

SOUTHWEST SCALLOP SALAD

SOUTHWEST SCALLOP SALAD

With lots of vegetables and a delicate seafood flavor, this colorful salad is ideal for a summer luncheon. A hint of lime draws out the garden goodness in the tomatoes and avocados, while the contrasting textures make each bite enjoyable.

—Marjorie Hennig, Green Valley, Arizona

1	pound bay scallops
1/4	cup lime juice
2	tablespoons olive oil
1-1/2	teaspoons sugar
1	teaspoon grated lime peel
1/4	teaspoon salt
1/8	teaspoon pepper
1	green onion, sliced
2	tablespoons minced fresh cilantro
1	teaspoon minced fresh parsley
1	medium ripe avocado, peeled and sliced
1/2	cup julienned roasted sweet red pepper
1	medium tomato, chopped
6	lettuce leaves
1	medium tomato, sliced

In a large saucepan, bring 3 in. of water to a boil. Reduce heat. Add scallops; simmer, uncovered, for 1-2 minutes or until scallops are firm and opaque. Drain immediately and rinse with cold water. Drain again.

In a large bowl, whisk the lime juice, oil, sugar, lime peel, salt and pepper. Stir in the green onion, cilantro and parsley. Dip avocado slices in lime juice mixture. Place on a plate; cover and refrigerate. Stir red peppers and scallops into lime juice mixture; cover and refrigerate for 1 hour or until chilled.

Just before serving, stir chopped tomato into lime juice mixture. Serve on lettuce leaf-lined individual plates with tomato and avocado slices. **Yield: 4 servings.**

COLORFUL BARLEY SALAD

Chili powder and cumin give this distinctive barley salad a subtle Tex-Mex spark. It is a super make-ahead side dish. Folks commented on how hearty and tasty it was when we served it at our wedding reception barbecue.

—Tracey Levreault, Baldur, Manitoba

3	cans (10-1/2 ounces *each*) condensed chicken broth, undiluted
4	cups water
3	cups medium pearl barley
1	cup canola oil
1/3	cup white vinegar
3	garlic cloves, minced
1-1/2	teaspoons chili powder
1-1/2	teaspoons ground cumin
6	large tomatoes, seeded and chopped
1	package (16 ounces) frozen corn
1	bunch green onions, sliced
1	cup minced fresh parsley

In a large soup kettle or Dutch oven, combine chicken broth and water; bring to a boil. Add barley; reduce heat. Cover and simmer for 35-40 minutes or until barley is tender. Cool slightly.

In a small bowl, combine the oil, vinegar, garlic, chili powder and cumin; pour over barley and toss well. Gently stir in the remaining ingredients. Transfer barley salad to a serving bowl; cover salad and refrigerate overnight. **Yield: 24 servings.**

COLORFUL BARLEY SALAD

GREEN CHILI RICE

GREEN CHILI RICE

With only five ingredients, this rich and creamy rice casserole mixes up in a snap. I always get requests for the recipe.

—Sandra Hanson, Emery, South Dakota

- 1 can (10-3/4 ounces) condensed cream of celery soup, undiluted
- 1 cup (8 ounces) sour cream
- 1 can (4 ounces) green chilies
- 1 cup (4 ounces) shredded cheddar cheese
- 1-1/2 cups uncooked instant rice

In a large bowl, combine the soup, sour cream, chilies and cheese. Stir in rice. Transfer to a greased shallow 1-1/2-qt. baking dish. Bake, uncovered, at 350° for 20 minutes or until rice is tender. **Yield: 4-6 servings.**

BLACK-EYED PEA AND BEAN SALAD

One day while I was trying to use up some ingredients I had in our pantry, I threw this bean salad together. I served it the next night with chicken, and everyone loved it.

—Marilyn Gonsman, Blairsville, Georgia

- 1 can (16 ounces) kidney beans, rinsed and drained
- 1 can (15-1/2 ounces) black-eyed peas, rinsed and drained
- 1 can (15 ounces) black beans, rinsed and drained
- 2 celery ribs, thinly sliced
- 1/2 cup chopped sweet red pepper
- 1/2 cup chopped red onion
- 3 tablespoons red wine vinegar
- 3 tablespoons white wine vinegar
- 2 tablespoons olive oil
- 1/2 teaspoon salt

In a large bowl, combine the kidney beans, black-eyed peas, black beans, celery, red pepper and onion. In a small bowl, whisk together the vinegars, oil and salt. Pour over bean mixture; toss to coat. Refrigerate for about 4 hours, stirring occasionally. **Yield: 8 servings.**

TACO PASTA SALAD

Two popular salads—taco and pasta—are blended into one satisfying side dish. Serve tortillas or corn chips on the side, and you have a complete meal.

—Gert Rosenau, Pewaukee, Wisconsin

- 2 cups uncooked spiral pasta
- 1 pound ground beef
- 1 envelope taco seasoning
- 3 cups shredded lettuce
- 2 cups halved cherry tomatoes
- 1 cup (4 ounces) shredded cheddar cheese
- 1/2 cup chopped onion
- 1/2 cup chopped green pepper
- 1/2 cup Catalina salad dressing
Tortilla chips

Cook pasta according to package directions. Meanwhile, in a large skillet, cook beef over medium heat until no longer pink; drain. Stir in the taco seasoning; cool.

Drain pasta and rinse in cold water; stir into meat mixture. Add the lettuce, tomatoes, cheese, onion, green pepper and dressing; toss to coat. Serve with tortilla chips. **Yield: 6 servings.**

TACO PASTA SALAD

SOUTHWEST PORK AND BEAN SALAD

HOT GREEN RICE

Our boys don't like spinach, except when it's served in this casserole. I think the jalapeno peppers disguise the veggie.

—Judy Brown, Rockdale, Texas

> 1/2 cup chopped onion
> 2 tablespoons butter
> 1 package (10 ounces) frozen chopped spinach, thawed and well drained
> 1 cup cooked rice
> 1 can (10-3/4 ounces) condensed cream of mushroom *or* chicken soup, undiluted
> 1/4 cup milk
> 2 jalapeno peppers, seeded and chopped
> 1/2 teaspoon salt
> 1/4 teaspoon pepper
> 4 ounces process cheese (Velveeta), cubed

In a large skillet, saute onion in butter until tender. Stir in spinach and rice. In a large bowl, combine the soup, milk, jalapeno, salt and pepper; add to spinach mixture and heat through. Stir in the cheese.

Pour into a greased 1-1/2-qt. baking dish. Bake, uncovered, at 350° for 25-30 minutes or until heated through. **Yield: 6 servings.**

Editor's Note: When cutting hot peppers, disposable gloves are recommended. Avoid touching your face.

SOUTHWEST PORK AND BEAN SALAD

This salad is scrumptious on its own, but we also like it as a filling for tacos or tortillas. Go ahead and substitute spicy shredded chicken for the pork to suit your family's tastes.

—Lynn Biscott, Toronto, Ontario

> 1 cup cubed cooked pork
> 1/2 medium sweet red pepper, chopped
> 3/4 cup frozen corn, thawed
> 1/2 cup canned kidney beans, rinsed and drained
> 1/4 cup chopped green onions
> 2 tablespoons balsamic vinegar
> 1 tablespoon water
> 1 tablespoon olive oil
> 1 garlic clove, minced
> 1/4 teaspoon salt
> 1/4 teaspoon pepper
> 1/4 teaspoon hot pepper sauce
> Lettuce leaves, optional

In a small bowl, combine the first five ingredients. In another bowl, whisk the vinegar, water, oil, garlic, salt, pepper and hot pepper sauce. Pour over pork mixture and toss to coat. Cover and refrigerate for at least 30 minutes. Serve salad on lettuce-lined plates if desired. **Yield: 2 servings.**

SOUTHWEST SKILLET CORN

This colorful stir-fried side complements any Mexican entree nicely. Enjoy it with everything from burritos to chimichangas. The fresh cilantro really shines through.

—Marilyn Smudzinski, Peru, Illinois

> 1 medium sweet red pepper, chopped
> 1 tablespoon finely chopped seeded jalapeno pepper
> 1 tablespoon butter
> 1-1/2 teaspoons ground cumin
> 1 package (16 ounces) frozen corn, thawed
> 1/3 cup minced fresh cilantro

In a large nonstick skillet, saute red pepper and jalapeno in butter until tender. Add cumin; cook for 30 seconds. Add corn and cilantro; saute 2 minutes longer or until heated through. **Yield: 4 servings.**

THREE-PEPPER CORN PUDDING

THREE-PEPPER CORN PUDDING

A trio of peppers livens up this comforting side dish. I've had this recipe for many years. I lightened it up from the original by using reduced-fat sour cream and milk, plus some egg substitute. It tastes just as good...but it's much better for us!

—Virginia Anthony, Jacksonville, Florida

1	medium sweet red pepper, chopped
6	green onions, thinly sliced
1	tablespoon olive oil
1	can (4 ounces) chopped green chilies, drained
3	medium jalapeno peppers, seeded and chopped
2	packages (10 ounces *each*) frozen corn, thawed, *divided*
1	can (12 ounces) reduced-fat evaporated milk
1/3	cup reduced-fat sour cream
1/4	cup fat-free milk
3	egg whites
2	eggs
1/4	cup cornstarch
1	teaspoon salt
1	teaspoon ground cumin
3/4	teaspoon ground thyme

In a nonstick skillet, saute the red pepper and onions in oil until tender. Remove from the heat. Stir in the chilies, jalapenos and half of the corn. Transfer to a 13-in. x 9-in. baking dish coated with cooking spray.

Easy Kitchen Tips

If you have to cut a large number of jalapeno peppers, try this time-saver:

First, cut off the tops of the peppers. Then slice them in half the long way. Use the small end of a melon baller to easily scrape out the seeds and membranes. Doing this speeds up the process and keeps you from accidentally slicing your gloves.

In a blender, combine the remaining ingredients; add remaining corn. Cover and process for 3 minutes or until smooth. Pour over red pepper mixture.

Bake, uncovered, at 350° for 45-50 minutes or until a knife inserted near the center comes out clean. **Yield: 12 servings.**

SPICY SPANISH RICE

This is a tasty dish to serve with a Southwestern-inspired meal or to perk up any ordinary dinner. We enjoy the slightly zesty combination with chicken enchiladas but I also prepare it for potlucks and family get-togethers. It's handy to not have to watch the rice cook on the stove.

—Marilyn Warner, Shirley, Arkansas

1	cup uncooked long grain rice
1	small onion, chopped
1	can (2-1/4 ounces) sliced ripe olives, drained
1	teaspoon ground cumin
2	cans (10 ounces *each*) diced tomatoes and green chilies, undrained
1	cup water
2	tablespoons canola oil
1	cup (4 ounces) shredded Monterey Jack cheese
2	tablespoons minced fresh cilantro, optional

In a greased 2-qt. baking dish, combine the rice, onion, olives, cumin, tomatoes, water and oil. Cover and bake at 350° for 45 minutes.

Stir in cheese. Bake, uncovered, 10-15 minutes longer or until rice is tender and liquid is absorbed. Stir in cilantro if desired. **Yield: 6-8 servings.**

SPICY SPANISH RICE

SALSA RICE WITH ZUCCHINI

SALSA RICE WITH ZUCCHINI

You won't create a mess in the kitchen with this recipe because the rice and zucchini are combined in one pan. For added color, do as our home economists did and toss in some diced yellow squash.

—Taste of Home Test Kitchen, Greendale, Wisconsin

  1   cup water
  1   tablespoon butter
  1   teaspoon beef bouillon granules
1/4 teaspoon ground cumin
1/8 teaspoon salt
  1   cup uncooked instant rice
  1   medium zucchini, diced
1/4 cup salsa

In a large saucepan, bring the water, butter, bouillon, cumin and salt to a boil. Remove from the heat; stir in the rice, zucchini and salsa. Cover and let stand for 5-7 minutes or until water is absorbed. Fluff with a fork. **Yield: 4 servings.**

CHEESY CHILI RELLENOS

I got this mouth-watering recipe in South Dakota. It also makes a good meatless main dish. I lived on a cattle ranch and cooked three meals a day, so I was always interested in finding new and different dishes to serve my family.

—Mary Morrow, Jordan Valley, Oregon

  3   cans (4 ounces *each*) whole green chilies, drained
1-1/2 cups (6 ounces) shredded Monterey jack cheese

1-1/2 cups (6 ounces) shredded cheddar cheese
1/3 cup all-purpose flour
  1   cup half-and-half cream
  2   eggs, lightly beaten
  1   can (8 ounces) tomato sauce

Cut chilies open lengthwise. Rinse; removing seeds. Place chilies on paper towels to drain. Combine cheeses; set aside 1/2 cup for topping. In a large bowl, combine the flour, cream and eggs until smooth.

In a greased deep 1-1/2-qt. baking dish, layer half of the cheese, chilies and egg mixture. Repeat layers. Pour tomato sauce over the top; sprinkle top with the reserved cheese.

Bake, uncovered, at 350° for 50-55 minutes or until knife inserted near the center comes out clean. Let stand for 5 minutes before serving. **Yield: 6-8 servings.**

Editor's Note: When cutting hot peppers, disposable gloves are recommended. Avoid touching your face.

BLACK BEAN FIESTA SALAD

This hearty, slightly spicy medley is always a winner. It's colorful, crunchy and easy to assemble.

—Bob Wedemeyer, Lynnwood, Washington

  1   can (15 ounces) black beans, rinsed and drained
  1   cup frozen corn, thawed
  1   green pepper, diced
  1   sweet red pepper, diced
  1   cup diced red onion
  2   celery ribs, chopped
3/4 cup cubed Monterey Jack cheese
  3   tablespoons lemon juice
  3   tablespoons red wine vinegar
  2   tablespoons olive oil
  2   garlic cloves, minced
  1   tablespoon Italian seasoning
  1   teaspoon pepper
1/2 teaspoon ground cumin

In a large bowl, combine the beans, corn, peppers, onion, celery and cheese. In a jar with a tight-fitting lid, combine the remaining ingredients; shake well. Pour dressing over vegetable mixture and toss gently to coat. Cover and chill for 2 hours or overnight. **Yield: 6 servings.**

SOUTHWESTERN VEGGIE SALAD

This speedy salad can be stirred up in absolutely no time. I enjoy making it because it takes so little effort and the bright veggies look simply striking on a buffet table.

—Rita Addicks, Weimar, Texas

- 2 cups whole kernel corn
- 1 small zucchini, sliced 1/4 inch thick
- 1 ripe avocado, peeled and chopped
- 1/4 cup thinly sliced radishes

Bibb *or* Boston lettuce leaves, optional
- 2 to 3 medium tomatoes, sliced

DRESSING:
- 3 tablespoons ketchup
- 2 tablespoons cider vinegar
- 1 tablespoon canola oil
- 1 tablespoon minced fresh cilantro
- 1/2 teaspoon garlic powder
- 1/4 teaspoon salt
- 1/4 teaspoon chili powder

In a large bowl, combine the corn, zucchini, avocado and radishes. On a serving plate, arrange lettuce if desired and tomatoes. In a small bowl, whisk the dressing ingredients. Pour over corn mixture; gently toss to coat. Spoon over tomatoes. **Yield: 5 servings.**

SOUTHWESTERN VEGGIE SALAD

TEX-MEX BEAN SALAD

TEX-MEX BEAN SALAD

Three kinds of beans, jalapeno peppers and a zesty blend of herbs and seasonings create this flavorful sensation. Using canned beans makes this dish both quick and convenient.

—Christi Gillentine, Tulsa, Oklahoma

- 1 can (16 ounces) kidney beans, rinsed and drained
- 1 can (15-1/2 ounces) red beans, rinsed and drained
- 1 can (15-1/2 ounces) black-eyed peas, rinsed and drained
- 1/4 cup minced fresh cilantro
- 1 jalapeno pepper, seeded and chopped
- 4 green onions, sliced
- 1/4 cup olive oil
- 1/4 cup red wine vinegar
- 1/2 teaspoon garlic salt
- 1/2 teaspoon pepper

In a large bowl, combine the first six ingredients. In a jar with a tight-fitting lid, combine the oil, vinegar, garlic salt and pepper; shake well.

Pour dressing over salad; toss to coat. Cover and refrigerate until serving. Serve with a slotted spoon. **Yield: 6 servings.**

Easy Kitchen Tips

Rinsing and draining canned beans before using in a recipe will remove extra salt from the canning process. If you choose to use the bean liquid, both the amount of salt and water in the recipe will need to be reduced.

Main Dishes

PINEAPPLE CHICKEN FAJITAS, P. 57

BELL PEPPER ENCHILADAS

BELL PEPPER ENCHILADAS

Peppers are probably the vegetable that gets used most frequently in my kitchen. My freezer is constantly stocked in case I discover a new recipe or want to whip up an old favorite. These zesty enchiladas are a standby that I make often for weeknight suppers throughout the year.

—Melissa Cowser, Greenville, Texas

    2   medium green peppers, chopped
  1/2   cup shredded cheddar cheese
  1/2   cup shredded Monterey Jack cheese
  1/2   cup process cheese (Velveeta)
    4   flour tortillas (8 inches), warmed
    1   small jalapeno pepper, minced, optional
    1   cup salsa, *divided*
Additional shredded cheese, optional

Sprinkle the green peppers and cheeses down the center of the tortillas; add jalapeno if desired. Roll up. Spread 1/2 cup salsa in a shallow baking dish. Place tortillas seam side down over salsa. Top with remaining salsa.

Bake enchiladas at 350° for 20 minutes or until heated through. Sprinkle with additional shredded cheese if desired. **Yield: 4 enchiladas.**

Editor's Note: When cutting hot peppers, disposable gloves are recommended. Avoid touching your face.

BEAN 'N' CHEESE BURRITOS

This is a recipe from my mom that I adapted to suit my taste. She made it with tortillas, but we both agree it's easier using frozen burritos. I make it about once each month.

—Karen Middleton, Elyria, Ohio

    8   frozen bean and cheese burritos (about
        5 ounces *each*), thawed
    1   can (10-3/4 ounces) condensed cream of
        chicken soup, undiluted
    1   can (10 ounces) enchilada sauce
  1/2   cup milk
    2   cups (8 ounces) shredded Mexican cheese
        blend *or* cheddar cheese, *divided*
    1   can (4 ounces) chopped green chilies
    1   cup sliced ripe olives
  1/2   cup sliced green onions
    6   cups shredded lettuce
Salsa and sour cream, optional

Arrange bean and cheese burritos in a greased 13-in. x 9-in. baking dish. In a large bowl, whisk the soup, sauce and milk until blended; stir in 1 cup of cheese and the chilies. Pour soup mixture over burritos. Sprinkle with the olives, green onions and remaining cheese.

Bake, uncovered, at 350° for 30-35 minutes or until bubbly and lightly browned. Serve the burritos on a bed of lettuce with salsa and sour cream if desired.
Yield: 6-8 servings.

BEAN 'N' CHEESE BURRITOS

PORK 'N' PEPPER TACOS

BEEF CHIMICHANGAS

A spicy sauce adds spark to these tasty beef-and-bean tortillas. I just fry them for a few minutes, sprinkle on some cheese and serve.
—Shelby Thompson, Camden Wyoming, Delaware

> 1 pound ground beef
> 1 can (16 ounces) refried beans
> 1/2 cup finely chopped onion
> 3 cans (8 ounces *each*) tomato sauce, *divided*
> 2 teaspoons chili powder
> 1 teaspoon minced garlic
> 1/2 teaspoon ground cumin
> 12 flour tortillas (10 inches), warmed
> 1 can (4 ounces) chopped green chilies
> 1 can (4 ounces) chopped jalapeno peppers

Oil for frying

> 1-1/2 cups (6 ounces) shredded cheddar cheese

In a large skillet, cook beef over medium heat until no longer pink; drain. Stir in the beans, onion, 1/2 cup tomato sauce, chili powder, garlic and cumin.

Spoon about 1/3 cup of beef mixture off-center on each tortilla. Fold edge nearest filling up and over to cover. Fold in both sides and roll up. Fasten with toothpicks. In a large saucepan, combine the chilies, jalapeno peppers and remaining tomato sauce; heat through.

In an electric skillet or deep-fat fryer, heat 1 in. of oil to 375°. Fry the chimichangas for 1-1/2 to 2 minutes on each side or until browned. Drain on paper towels. Serve with sauce. Sprinkle with cheese. **Yield: 1 dozen.**

Editor's Note: Chimichangas may be baked instead of fried. To bake, brush with melted butter and bake at 350° for 25-30 minutes or until golden brown (if frozen, thaw chimichangas before baking).

PORK 'N' PEPPER TACOS

As a Texas native, I prefer spicy food. But since my husband and I both work nights, I also need quick dishes that don't require a lot of fuss. These deliciously different tacos have always been well received.
—Jacquie Baldwin, Raleigh, North Carolina

> 1 medium onion, chopped
> 2 medium jalapeno peppers, diced
> 3 tablespoons canola oil
> 2 pounds boneless pork, cut into bite-size pieces
> 1 tablespoon chili powder
> 1/2 teaspoon salt
> 1/4 teaspoon pepper
> 8 taco shells, warmed

Shredded lettuce, cheddar cheese, chopped tomato and salsa

In a large skillet, saute onion and jalapenos in oil for 3-4 minutes or until tender. Add the pork; cook and stir over medium heat for about 8 minutes or until the meat is no longer pink.

Stir in the chili powder, salt and pepper. Reduce heat; cover and simmer for 25-30 minutes or until the meat is tender, stirring occasionally.

Serve in taco shells with lettuce, cheese, tomato and salsa. **Yield: 8 tacos.**

Editor's Note: When cutting hot peppers, disposable gloves are recommended. Avoid touching your face.

BEEF CHIMICHANGAS

PINEAPPLE CHICKEN FAJITAS

PINEAPPLE CHICKEN FAJITAS

Honey and pineapple add a sweet twist to these fajitas that my family loves. I like to serve them with sour cream, shredded cheddar cheese, salsa and toasted almonds as toppings.
—Raymonde Bourgeois, Swastika, Ontario

2	pounds boneless skinless chicken breasts, cut into strips
1	tablespoon olive oil
1	each medium green, sweet red and yellow pepper, julienned
1	medium onion, cut into thin wedges
2	tablespoons fajita seasoning mix
1/4	cup water
2	tablespoons honey
1	tablespoon dried parsley flakes
1	teaspoon garlic powder
1/2	teaspoon salt
1/2	cup unsweetened pineapple chunks, drained
8	flour tortillas (10 inches), warmed

In a large nonstick skillet, cook chicken in oil for 4-5 minutes. Add peppers and onion; cook and stir 4-5 minutes longer.

In a small bowl, combine seasoning mix and water; stir in the honey, parsley, garlic powder and salt. Stir into skillet. Add pineapple. Cook and stir for 1-2 minutes or until chicken juices run clear and vegetables are tender.

Place chicken mixture on one side of each tortilla; fold tortillas over filling. **Yield: 8 fajitas.**

GREEN CHILI FLAUTAS

This recipe has always been a great success at potlucks, especially when we lived in New Mexico. You can also assemble this dish ahead of time and freeze it to bake at a later date.
—Lisa Ann Platt, Bellevue, Nebraska

1-1/2	pounds ground beef
1	cup (4 ounces) shredded cheddar cheese
1	can (4 ounces) chopped green chilies, drained
1/2	teaspoon ground cumin
10	flour tortillas (6 inches)
1/3	cup butter, melted, *divided*

Shredded lettuce, guacamole, salsa and sour cream

In a large skillet, cook beef over medium heat until no longer pink; drain. Add the cheese, chilies and cumin; set aside.

Warm the tortillas; brush both sides with some of the butter. Spoon about 1/3 cup beef mixture down the center of each tortilla. Roll up tightly; place seam side down in a greased 13-in. x 9-in. baking pan.

Bake, uncovered, at 500° for 5-7 minutes or until golden brown, brushing once with remaining butter. Serve with toppings of your choice. **Yield: 10 flautas.**

Editor's Note: To quickly warm flour tortillas, place unwrapped tortillas on a microwave-safe plate and cover with a microwave-safe paper towel. Microwave on high for 30-60 seconds or until warm.

GREEN CHILI FLAUTAS

ASPARAGUS CHICKEN FAJITAS

ASPARAGUS CHICKEN FAJITAS

When my children visited their aunt, she served these colorful fajitas. They were so impressed, they brought the recipe home to me. It's a great way to get them to eat vegetables.
—Marlene Mohr, Cincinnati, Ohio

  1   pound boneless skinless chicken breasts, cut into strips
3/4   cup fat-free Italian salad dressing
  1   tablespoon canola oil
  1   pound fresh asparagus, trimmed and cut into 2-inch pieces
  1   medium sweet red pepper, julienned
  1   medium sweet yellow pepper, julienned
1/2   cup fresh or frozen corn
1/4   cup diced onion
  2   tablespoons lemon juice
1/2   teaspoon garlic salt
1/8   teaspoon pepper
 12   flour tortillas (6 inches), warmed

Place chicken in a large resealable plastic bag; add salad dressing. Seal bag and turn to coat; refrigerate for 4 hours, turning several times.

Drain and discard marinade. In a large nonstick skillet, saute chicken in oil for 3 minutes. Add the asparagus, peppers, corn and onion. Cook, uncovered for 7 minutes or until the chicken juices run clear and vegetables are crisp-tender, stirring occasionally. Stir in the lemon juice, garlic salt and pepper. Spoon 1/2 cup on each tortilla; fold in sides. **Yield: 6 servings.**

SWEET 'N' SAVORY ENCHILADAS

Whenever my husband has a potluck at the office, he signs me up to bring these saucy enchiladas.
—GaleLynn Peterson, Long Beach, California

  1   can (14-1/2 ounces) whole tomatoes, undrained
  2   medium onions, cut into wedges
  2   garlic cloves
1-1/2 teaspoons dried oregano
1-1/4 teaspoon salt
  1   teaspoon pepper
1/2   teaspoon ground cumin
4-1/2 teaspoons canola oil
  1   cup heavy whipping cream
  2   pounds ground beef
  1   pound bulk pork sausage
 12   flour tortillas (8 inches), warmed
3/4   cup shredded Colby cheese
1/2   cup shredded Monterey Jack cheese
1/2   cup thinly sliced green onions

In a blender, combine tomatoes, onions, garlic and seasonings. Cover and process until blended. Transfer to a saucepan. Add oil. Bring to a boil. Cook and stir for 3 minutes or until thickened.

Remove from the heat. Gradually add a small amount of hot tomato mixture to cream, stirring constantly. Return all to pan; set aside.

In a large skillet, cook beef and sausage over medium heat until meat is no longer pink; drain. Stir in 2/3 cup of the tomato cream sauce.

Spoon meat mixture onto tortillas. Roll up and place seam side down in a baking dish. Pour remaining sauce over enchilada. Bake, uncovered, at 350° for 20 minutes or until heated through. Sprinkle with cheeses. Bake 10 minutes longer or until cheese is melted. Sprinkle with onions. **Yield: 12 enchiladas.**

Easy Kitchen Tips

Purchase green onions with fresh-looking tops and clean white ends. Wrap and store in the refrigerator for up to 5 days. For longer storage, freeze sliced or chopped green onions for up to 1 year. One green onion equals about 2 tablespoons sliced.

SAUSAGE FAJITAS

SAUSAGE FAJITAS

The secret to these fajitas is the speedy herbal marinade. To save even more time, I marinate everything the night before.
—Janie McClellan, Ocean Isle Beach, North Carolina

1	cup reduced-sodium chicken broth
1/4	cup olive oil
1/4	cup red wine vinegar
1/4	cup reduced-sodium soy sauce
1/4	cup Worcestershire sauce
1	tablespoon *each* dried basil, oregano and thyme
1/4	teaspoon pepper
3/4	pound smoked turkey kielbasa, sliced
3	cups julienned mixed sweet peppers
1	medium red onion, thinly sliced
1	cup sliced fresh mushrooms
4	whole wheat tortillas (8 inches), warmed
4	tablespoons fat-free sour cream
1	small tomato, chopped

In a large resealable plastic bag, combine the broth, oil, vinegar, soy sauce, Worcestershire sauce, herbs and pepper; add the sausage, peppers, onion and mushrooms. Seal bag and turn to coat; refrigerate for at least 2 hours.

Drain marinade, reserving 1/2 cup. In a large nonstick skillet, cook sausage and vegetables in reserved marinade for 9-11 minutes or until sausage is heated through and vegetables are tender. Spoon sausage mixture over half of each tortilla; top with sour cream and tomato. Fold over. **Yield: 4 servings.**

SALMON QUESADILLAS

I like simple recipes that get me out of the kitchen fast, so my husband and I can spend more time with our two sons. These super-quick wedges are a favorite of our boys...and a tasty change of pace from salmon patties.
—Heidi Main, Anchorage, Alaska

2	garlic cloves, minced
1	teaspoon canola oil
1	can (14-3/4 ounces) salmon, drained, bones and skin removed
1	to 2 teaspoons dried basil
1/2	teaspoon pepper
1	tablespoon butter, softened
4	flour tortillas (8 inches), warmed
2	cups (8 ounces) part-skim shredded mozzarella cheese

Guacamole *or* salsa

In a small skillet, saute garlic in oil until tender. Stir in the salmon, basil and pepper. Cook over medium heat until heated through.

Meanwhile, spread butter over one side of each tortilla; place buttered side down on a griddle. Sprinkle 1/4 cup cheese over half of each tortilla; top with salmon mixture and remaining cheese.

Fold tortilla over filling. Cook over low heat for 1-2 minutes on each side or until cheese is melted. Cut each tortilla into three wedges; serve with guacamole or salsa.
Yield: 4 servings.

SALMON QUESADILLAS

JALAPENO CHICKEN ENCHILADAS

JALAPENO CHICKEN ENCHILADAS

These enchiladas are likely to be as popular at your house as they are at mine. The creamy filling and slight bite make them a frequent request. For weddings, I place the recipe in a nice casserole dish to give as a unique gift.

—Kaylin DeVries, Magna, Utah

2	cans (15 ounces *each*) tomato sauce, *divided*
4	cans (10-3/4 ounces *each*) condensed cream of chicken soup, undiluted
4	cups (32 ounces) sour cream
4	jalapeno peppers, seeded and chopped
1	teaspoon onion salt
1/4	teaspoon pepper
4	cups cubed cooked chicken
3	cups (12 ounces) shredded cheddar cheese, *divided*
20	flour tortilla (8 inches), warmed

In each of two greased 13-in. x 9-in. baking dishes, spread 1/2 cup of tomato sauce; set aside. In a large bowl, combine the soup, sour cream, jalapenos, onion salt and pepper. Stir in chicken and 2 cups cheese.

Spread about 1/2 cup chicken mixture down the center of each tortilla. Roll up and place seam side down in prepared dishes. Top with remaining tomato sauce; sprinkle with the remaining cheese.

Cover and bake one casserole at 350° for 35-45 minutes or until edges are bubbly. Cover and freeze remaining casserole for up to 1 month. **Yield: 2 casseroles (5 servings each).**

To use frozen casserole: Thaw in the refrigerator overnight. Bake, covered, at 350° for 40-45 minutes or until edges are bubbly.

Editor's Note: *When cutting hot peppers, disposable gloves are recommended. Avoid touching your face.*

CHEESY CHIMICHANGAS

When I was growing up, our family would travel from our home in New York to visit Grandma in Arizona. That's where I first sampled these can't-be-beat chimichangas. Now I serve them to my family who enjoys them just as much.

—Deborah Martin, Grand Prairie, Texas

1-1/2	pounds ground beef
2	large onions, chopped
2	teaspoon garlic salt
1/2	teaspoon pepper
12	flour tortillas (6 inches), warmed

Canola oil

1	jar (16 ounces) salsa, *divided*
2	cups (8 ounces) shredded cheddar cheese, *divided*
2	cups (8 ounces) shredded Monterey Jack cheese, *divided*

Shredded lettuce and chopped tomatoes
Sour cream and guacamole, optional

In a large skillet, cook the ground beef and onions over medium heat until meat is no longer pink; drain. Stir in garlic salt and pepper.

Brush one side of each tortilla with oil. Spoon 1/4 cup beef mixture off-center on oiled side of tortillas. Top with 1 tablespoon each of salsa, cheddar cheese and Monterey Jack cheese. Fold sides and ends over filling and roll up. Secure with toothpicks; place in a greased 13-in. x 9-in. baking dish. Brush with oil.

Bake, uncovered, at 450° for 10-15 minutes or until lightly browned. Sprinkle chimichangas with remaining cheeses. Bake 2-3 minutes longer or until cheese is melted. Remove the toothpicks.

Serve the chimichangas with shredded lettuce and tomato. Spoon the remaining salsa over chimichangas. Serve the chimichangas with sour cream and guacamole if desired. **Yield: 1 dozen.**

Editor's Note: *Keep a batch of Cheesy Chimichangas in the freezer. Assemble as directed and freeze in an airtight container up to 3 months. Thaw in the refrigerator, brush with oil and bake as directed.*

GRILLED PORK AND POBLANO PEPPERS

GRILLED PORK AND POBLANO PEPPERS

We entertain a lot in summer, and this has quickly become the most-requested dish, served with Mexican rice and salad.
—Donna Gay Harris, Springdale, Arkansas

    4   large poblano peppers
    2   cups (8 ounces) shredded Monterey Jack
        cheese
4-1/2   teaspoons chili powder
1-1/2   teaspoons *each* onion powder and ground cumin
  1/2   teaspoon garlic powder
  1/4   teaspoon salt
  1/8   teaspoon aniseed, ground
  1/8   teaspoon cayenne pepper
    2   pork tenderloins (about 1 pound *each*)

Cut the top off each pepper and set tops aside. Remove seeds. Stuff peppers with cheese. Replace tops and secure with toothpicks; set aside.

Combine the seasonings; rub over pork. Grill, covered, over medium-hot heat for 18 minutes or until a meat thermometer reads 160°. Place peppers on sides of grill (not directly over coals); heat for 10 minutes or until browned. **Yield: 6-8 servings.**

TILAPIA WITH CORN SALSA

My family loves fish, and this no-fuss, delicious entree is very popular at my house. Though it tastes like it takes a long time, it cooks in just minutes under the broiler.
—Brenda Coffey, Singer Island, Florida

    4   tilapia fillets (6 ounces *each*)
    1   tablespoon olive oil
  1/4   teaspoon salt
  1/4   teaspoon pepper
    1   can (15 ounces) black beans, rinsed and
        drained
    1   can (11 ounces) whole kernel corn, drained
  3/4   cup Italian salad dressing
    2   tablespoons chopped green onion
    2   tablespoons chopped sweet red pepper

Drizzle both sides of tilapia fillets with oil; sprinkle fillets with salt and pepper.

Broil fillets 4-6 in. from the heat for 5-7 minutes or until the fish flakes easily with a fork. Meanwhile, in a small bowl, combine the remaining ingredients. Serve with fish.
Yield: 4 servings.

CORNY CHICKEN WRAPS

My girls like these tortilla roll-ups very much—in fact, they'll ask for them practically every week! Tender chicken mixes with canned corn and salsa for a fast-to-fix main dish.
—Sue Seymour, Valatie, New York

    2   cups cubed cooked chicken breast
    1   can (11 ounces) whole kernel corn, drained
    1   cup salsa
    1   cup (4 ounces) shredded cheddar cheese
    8   flour tortillas (6 inches), warmed

In a large saucepan, combine the chicken, corn and salsa. Cook over medium heat until heated through.

Sprinkle cheese over tortillas. Place about 1/2 cup chicken mixture down the center of each tortilla; roll up. Secure with toothpicks. **Yield: 4 servings.**

CORNY CHICKEN WRAPS

ARROZ CON POLLO

ARROZ CON POLLO

Translated to mean "rice with chicken," this authentic Mexican specialty developed by our home economists gets its wonderful flavor from a robust blend of seasonings including garlic, Mexican oregano and chili powder.

—Taste of Home Test Kitchen, Greendale, Wisconsin

1	can (14-1/2 ounces) diced tomatoes, drained
1/2	cup chopped onion
4	garlic cloves, peeled
1	teaspoon salt, *divided*
1/2	teaspoon dried Mexican oregano
1/2	teaspoon chili powder
1/2	teaspoon pepper, *divided*
1	broiler/fryer chicken (3 to 4 pounds), cut up
3	tablespoons canola oil, *divided*
1-1/2	cups uncooked long grain rice
3	cups chicken broth
1	cup frozen peas

In a blender, combine the tomatoes, onion, garlic, 1/2 teaspoon salt, oregano, chili powder and 1/4 teaspoon pepper; cover and process until smooth. Set aside.

Sprinkle chicken with remaining salt and pepper. In a large skillet over medium heat, cook the chicken in batches in 2 tablespoons oil for 10 minutes or until lightly browned. Remove and keep warm. In the same skillet, saute the rice for 2 minutes or until lightly browned. Stir in chicken broth.

In a Dutch oven, heat the remaining oil; add tomato mixture. Bring to a boil; cook and stir for 4 minutes. Stir in rice mixture; bring to a boil.

Arrange chicken in pan. Reduce heat to medium; cover and cook for 25-30 minutes or until the rice is tender and the chicken juices run clear. Stir in peas; cover and let stand for 4 minutes or until the peas are heated through. **Yield: 5-6 servings.**

CHICKEN VEGGIE FAJITAS

Our family loves these speedy fajitas that sizzle with fresh Southwestern flair. The seasoned meat and veggies wrapped in warm tortillas beat any restaurant version.

—Eleanor Martens, Rosenort, Manitoba

3	tablespoons lemon juice
1	tablespoon soy sauce
1	tablespoon Worcestershire sauce
2	teaspoons canola oil
1	garlic clove, minced
1/2	teaspoon ground cumin
1/2	teaspoon dried oregano
3/4	pound boneless skinless chicken breasts, cut into 1/2-inch strips
1	small onion, sliced and separated into rings
1/2	*each* medium green, sweet red and yellow pepper, julienned
4	flour tortillas (6 inches), warmed

Shredded cheddar cheese, optional

In a small bowl, combine the first seven ingredients. Place the chicken and vegetables in a single layer in a greased 15-in. x 10-in. baking pan; drizzle with 1/4 cup lemon juice mixture. Broil 4-6 in. from the heat for 4 minutes.

Turn chicken and vegetables; drizzle with remaining lemon juice mixture. Broil 4 minutes longer or until chicken juices run clear. Serve on tortillas with cheese if desired. **Yield: 4 servings.**

CHICKEN VEGGIE FAJITAS

PEPPER STEAK QUESADILLAS

PEPPER STEAK QUESADILLAS

I came up with this savory entree when my family needed a quick meal before running off in several directions. I threw together what I had in the fridge, and it was a winner.

—Barbara Moore, Farmington, New Mexico

- 1/2   pound boneless beef sirloin steak
- 1/2   *each* medium green, sweet red and yellow pepper, julienned
- 1   tablespoon chopped red onion
- 1   garlic clove, minced
- 1   tablespoon minced fresh cilantro
- 1/4   teaspoon dried rosemary, crushed
- 4   flour tortillas (6 inches)
- 6   cherry tomatoes, halved
- 1/4   cup sliced fresh mushrooms
- 1   cup (4 ounces) shredded part-skim mozzarella cheese

If grilling the steak, coat grill rack with cooking spray before starting the grill. Grill steak, covered, over medium heat or broil 4 in. from the heat for 4-6 minutes on each side or until meat reaches desired doneness (for medium-rare, a meat thermometer should read 145°; medium, 160°; well-done, 170°). Let stand for 10 minutes.

Meanwhile, in a large skillet coated with cooking spray, saute the peppers, onion and garlic for 5-6 minutes or until tender. Sprinkle with cilantro and rosemary.

Place two tortillas on a baking sheet coated with cooking spray. Cut steak into thin strips; place on tortillas. Using a slotted spoon, place pepper mixture over steak. Top with tomatoes, mushrooms, cheese and remaining tortillas; lightly spray top of tortillas with cooking spray.

Bake at 425° for 5-10 minutes or until golden brown and cheese is melted. Cut each quesadilla into four wedges. **Yield: 4 servings.**

DOUBLE-SHELL TACOS

Two-shell tacos are twice the fun. A warm pita spread with refried beans enfolds a crispy taco shell filled with mouth-watering beef and tempting toppings for this casual entree.
    —Taste of Home Test Kitchen, Greendale, Wisconsin

- 1/2   pound ground beef
- 2   tablespoons taco seasoning
- 1/3   cup water
- 1/2   cup refried beans
- 2   whole gyro-style pitas (6 inches)
- 2   taco shells

Toppings: chopped green onions, chopped tomatoes, sliced ripe olives, shredded cheddar cheese, sour cream *and/or* shredded lettuce, optional

In a large skillet, cook beef over medium heat until no longer pink; drain. Stir in taco seasoning and water. Bring to a boil. Reduce heat; simmer, uncovered, for 3-4 minutes or until thickened.

Meanwhile, spread 1/4 cup refried beans over one side of each pita. Place on a microwave-safe plate; heat, uncovered, on high for 15-20 seconds or until warmed. Immediately wrap each pita around a taco shell. Fill taco shell with beef mixture. Serve with toppings of your choice. **Yield: 2 servings.**

Editor's Note: This recipe was tested in a 1,100-watt microwave.

DOUBLE-SHELL TACOS

GRILLED FAJITAS

MOLE POBLANO DE GUAJOLOTE

Mole Poblano, a traditional Spanish sauce, gives tender turkey real authentic Southwestern flavor in this pleasing entree.
—Taste of Home Test Kitchen, Greendale, Wisconsin

1	turkey (8 to 10 pounds)
1-1/2	teaspoons salt
1/3	cup lard
4	cups Mole Poblano (recipe on p. 10)
1/4	cup sesame seeds, toasted

Pat turkey dry. Cut off wings; discard or save for another use. Cut off legs; separate drumsticks from thighs. Cut the breast into quarters. Sprinkle all sides of turkey pieces with salt. In a Dutch oven or large heavy skillet, melt lard. Cook turkey pieces in batches over medium heat until browned on all sides. Remove and keep warm.

Drain pan drippings. Return turkey to Dutch oven. Pour mole over the top; bring to a boil. Reduce heat; cover and simmer for 1 hour or until a meat thermometer reads 180°.

Remove turkey to a cutting board; cover and let stand for 15 minutes. Cut turkey into 1/4-in. slices if desired. Arrange turkey slices or pieces in a deep serving dish; drizzle with mole. Sprinkle turkey with toasted sesame seeds. **Yield: 6-8 servings.**

GRILLED FAJITAS

A special marinade gives the meat in these fajitas outstanding flavor that's always a hit. It's a satisfying main dish that makes use of garden-fresh peppers and onions.
—Cheryl Smith, The Dalles, Oregon

1	envelope onion soup mix
1/4	cup canola oil
1/4	cup lime juice
1/4	cup water
2	garlic cloves, minced
1	teaspoon grated lime peel
1	teaspoon ground cumin
1/2	teaspoon dried oregano
1/4	teaspoon pepper
1	beef flank steak (about 1 pound)
1	medium onion, thinly sliced
	Green, sweet red *and/or* yellow peppers, julienned
1	tablespoon canola oil
8	flour tortillas (8 inches), warmed

In a large resealable plastic bag, combine the first nine ingredients; add steak. Seal bag; turn to coat. Cover and refrigerate 4 hours or overnight.

Drain and discard the marinade. Grill meat over high heat until the meat reaches desired doneness (for medium-rare, a meat thermometer should read 145°; medium, 160°; well-done, 170°).

Meanwhile, in a small skillet, saute onion and peppers if desired in oil for 3-4 minute or until crisp-tender. Slice meat into thin strips across the grain; place on tortillas. Top with vegetables; roll up. **Yield: 4 servings.**

MOLE POBLANO DE GUAJOLOTE

Easy Kitchen Tips

Here are some helpful tips for grilling the perfect steak. Trim the steak to avoid flare-ups, leaving a thin layer of fat if desired to maintain juiciness. Then, pat the steak dry with paper towels before grilling—a dry steak will brown better than a moist one. Also, avoid grilling at too high a temperature to prevent charring.

STEAK TORTILLAS

STEAK TORTILLAS

When I fix steak, I always grill one extra so I have leftovers to make these delicious filled tortillas. The steak strips are seasoned with salsa, chili powder and cumin, then tucked inside soft flour tortillas with tasty toppings.

—Kris Wells, Hereford, Arizona

  2   cups thinly sliced cooked beef rib eye steak (about 3/4 pound)
  1   small onion, chopped
1/4   cup salsa
1/2   teaspoon ground cumin
1/2   teaspoon chili powder
1/4   teaspoon garlic powder
1-1/2   teaspoons all-purpose flour
1/2   cup cold water
  6   flour tortillas (8 inches), warmed
Shredded cheese, chopped lettuce and tomatoes and additional salsa, optional

In a large nonstick skillet, saute the steak and onion until meat is no longer pink; drain. Stir in the salsa, cumin, chili powder and garlic powder.

In a small bowl, combine flour and water until smooth; gradually add to the skillet. Bring to a boil; cook and stir for 1-2 minutes or until thickened. Place on tortillas; top with cheese, lettuce, tomatoes and additional salsa if desired. Fold in sides. **Yield: 6 servings.**

SPINACH CHICKEN ENCHILADAS

My husband is a pastor, so I fix meals for large groups often. This hearty specialty is a favorite, and offers a nice alternative from the usual beef enchiladas.

—Joy Headley, Grand Prairie, Texas

  4   boneless skinless chicken breast halves, cut into thin strips
1/4   cup chopped onion
  1   package (10 ounces) frozen chopped spinach, thawed and well drained
  1   can (10-3/4 ounces) condensed cream of mushroom soup, undiluted
3/4   cup milk
  1   cup (8 ounces) sour cream
  1   teaspoon ground nutmeg
  1   teaspoon garlic powder
  1   teaspoon onion powder
  8   flour tortillas (8 inches)
  2   cups (8 ounces) shredded part-skim mozzarella cheese
Minced fresh parsley

Coat a large skillet with cooking spray; cook and stir chicken and onion over medium heat for 6-8 minutes or until chicken juices run clear. Remove from the heat; stir in the chopped spinach.

In a large bowl, combine the soup, milk, sour cream and seasonings. Stir 3/4 cup soup mixture into chicken mixture. Place filling down the center of each tortilla. Roll up and place, seam side down, in a 13-in. x 9-in. baking pan that has been sprayed with cooking spray. Pour the remaining soup mixture over enchiladas.

Cover and bake at 350° for 30 minutes. Uncover and sprinkle with cheese; bake 15 minutes longer or until cheese is melted and bubbly. Garnish enchiladas with parsley. **Yield: 8 servings.**

SPINACH CHICKEN ENCHILADAS

PORK FAJITA KABOBS

PORK FAJITA KABOBS

This has become my favorite way to cook pork loin. The grilled vegetable and meat chunks, seasoned with a homemade, Southwestern-style spice blend, are appropriately served in a flour tortilla. Just top with salsa and enjoy.

—Bea Westphal, Slidell, Louisiana

2	teaspoons paprika
1-1/2	teaspoons ground cumin
1-1/2	teaspoons dried oregano
1	teaspoon garlic powder
1/8	to 1/4 teaspoon crushed red pepper flakes
1-1/2	pounds boneless pork loin chops, cut into 1-inch cubes
1	small green pepper, cut into 1-inch pieces
1	small onion, cut into eight wedges
8	large fresh mushrooms
16	grape tomatoes
8	flour tortillas (8 inches), warmed
3/4	cup chunky salsa

In a large resealable plastic bag, combine the paprika, cumin, oregano, garlic powder and pepper flakes; add pork. Seal bag and toss to coat. On eight metal or soaked wooden skewers, alternately thread the pork, green pepper, onion, mushrooms and tomatoes.

Grill kabobs, covered, over medium heat for 5-8 minutes on each side or until meat is no longer pink and vegetables are tender. Place each kabob in a tortilla; remove skewers and fold tortillas in half. Serve with salsa. **Yield: 4 servings.**

CHICKEN QUESADILLAS

You'll love these melty, gooey quesadillas stuffed with chicken, cheese, green onions and seasonings. They come together quickly for a simple, family-pleasing meal.

—Linda Wetzel, Woodland Park, Colorado

2-1/2	cups shredded cooked chicken
2/3	cup salsa
1/3	cup sliced green onions
3/4	to 1 teaspoon ground cumin
1/2	teaspoon salt
1/2	teaspoon dried oregano
6	flour tortillas (8 inches)
1/4	cup butter, melted
2	cups (8 ounces) shredded Monterey Jack cheese

Sour cream and guacamole

In a skillet, combine the first six ingredients. Cook, uncovered, over medium heat for 10 minutes or until heated through, stirring occasionally.

Brush one side of tortillas with butter; place buttered side down on a lightly greased baking sheet. Spoon 1/3 cup chicken mixture over half of each tortilla; sprinkle with 1/3 cup cheese.

Fold plain side of tortilla over cheese. Bake at 475° for 10 minutes or until crisp and golden brown. Cut into wedges; serve with sour cream and guacamole. **Yield: 6 servings.**

CHICKEN QUESADILLAS

TEX-MEX TURKEY TACOS

TEX-MEX TURKEY TACOS

I normally don't care for ground turkey, but I love the fresh
Southwestern taste of the well-seasoned taco meat mixed with
peppers, onions and black beans. One bite of these crunchy
tacos is sure to make them a hit at your house.

—Jodi Fleury, West Gardiner, Maine

1	pound lean ground turkey
2	medium green peppers, chopped
1	medium sweet red pepper, chopped
1	medium onion, chopped
2	medium carrots, halved lengthwise and sliced
2	garlic cloves, minced
1	tablespoon olive oil
2	cans (15 ounces *each*) black beans, rinsed and drained
1	jar (16 ounces) salsa
2	tablespoons chili powder
1	tablespoon ground cumin
24	taco shells
3	cups shredded lettuce
1-1/2	cups diced fresh tomato
1/2	cup minced fresh cilantro

In a large nonstick skillet coated with cooking spray, cook
turkey over medium heat until no longer pink; remove and
set aside. In the same skillet, saute the peppers, onion,
carrots and garlic in oil for 8-10 minutes or until
vegetables are tender.

Add the turkey, beans, salsa, chili powder and cumin;
bring to a boil. Reduce heat; simmer, uncovered, for 10-15
minutes or until thickened. Fill each taco shell with 1/3
cup turkey mixture. Serve with lettuce, tomato and
cilantro. **Yield: 12 servings.**

VEGGIE BROWN RICE WRAPS

Salsa gives a bit of zip to the brown rice and bean filling in
these meatless tortilla wraps. It's a delicious alternative to
traditional meat-filled burritos and soft tacos.

—Lisa Sullivan, St. Mary's, Ohio

1	medium sweet red *or* green pepper, diced
1	cup sliced fresh mushrooms
2	garlic cloves, minced
1	tablespoon olive oil
2	cups cooked brown rice
1	can (16 ounces) kidney beans, rinsed and drained
1	cup frozen corn, thawed
1/4	cup chopped green onions
1/2	teaspoon ground cumin
1/2	teaspoon pepper
1/4	teaspoon salt
6	flour tortillas (8 inches), room temperature
1/2	cup shredded reduced-fat cheddar cheese
3/4	cup salsa

In a large nonstick skillet, saute the pepper, mushrooms
and garlic in oil until tender. Add the rice, beans, corn,
green onions, cumin, pepper and salt. Cook and stir for 4-
6 minutes or until heated through.

Spoon 3/4 cup onto each tortilla. Sprinkle with cheese;
drizzle with salsa. Fold sides of tortilla over filling; serve
immediately. **Yield: 6 servings.**

VEGGIE BROWN RICE WRAPS

CRISPY FRIED TACOS

CRISPY FRIED TACOS

My mother has been making these for more than 30 years. Frying the filled tacos makes them extra crispy and delicious. Our five grown sons request these whenever they visit.
—Catherine Gibbs, Gambrills, Maryland

SALSA:
- 1 can (28 ounces) diced tomatoes, undrained
- 1 can (8 ounces) tomato sauce
- 1 can (4 ounces) sliced jalapeno peppers
- 1 small onion, quartered
- 1 teaspoon garlic salt

TACOS:
- 1 pound ground beef
- 1/2 teaspoon salt
- 1/2 cup canola oil
- 12 corn tortillas (6 inches), warmed
- 1 cup (4 ounces) shredded cheddar cheese
- 4 cups shredded lettuce

In a blender, combine the salsa ingredients; cover and pulse until salsa reaches desired consistency. Transfer to a large bowl; cover and refrigerate.

In a large skillet, cook beef over medium heat until no longer pink; drain. Sprinkle with salt. Meanwhile in another large skillet, fry tortillas in oil just until softened; drain on paper towels.

Fill tortillas with beef; sprinkle with cheese. Fold in half. In an ungreased skillet, fry tortillas on both sides until crisp. Serve with lettuce and salsa. **Yield: 12 tacos.**

Editor's Note: *When cutting hot peppers, disposable gloves are recommended. Avoid touching your face.*

TAMALES

Tamales are a traditional Mexican dish. Yummy packets of corn dough have a savory or sweet filling and are typically wrapped in corn husks or banana leaves. Because they take awhile to make, tamales are served more for special occasions and holidays than as everyday fare.
—Jacquelynne Stine, Las Vegas, Nevada

- 1 boneless pork shoulder roast (4 pounds)
- 4 cups water
- 1 cup finely chopped onion
- 1/3 cup adobo sauce
- 1/4 cup chili sauce
- 2 dried guajillo chilies
- 1/4 cup lime juice
- 4 garlic cloves, peeled
- 32 corn husks

FILLING:
- 7 cups maseca cornmeal
- 9 teaspoons baking powder
- 3 teaspoons salt
- 4 cups warm water (110° to 115°)
- 1-1/2 cups butter-flavored shortening

Place the first eight ingredients in a Dutch oven. Cover and bake at 325° for 3-4 hours or until the pork roast is very tender.

Meanwhile, place corn husks in a large kettle; cover with cold water and soak for at least 2 hours.

Remove roast and shred meat with two forks; set aside and keep warm. Skim fat from pan juices; discard chilies. Bring to a boil; cook until liquid is reduced to 4 cups.

For filling, in a large bowl, combine the cornmeal, baking powder and salt; beat in water, 2 cups pan juices and shortening just until combined (bowl will be full). Refrigerate remaining pan juices.

Drain corn husks and pat dry. (Until ready to use, keep husks covered with plastic wrap and a damp towel to prevent them from drying out.) Spread 3 tablespoons filling over each husk to within 1/4 in. of edges. Top each with 1/4 cup pork and 3 tablespoons filling. Using the husk to lift one long side, roll up filling. Enclose filling with husk; fold bottom end of husk over the top.

In a large steamer basket, position tamales upright with folded bottoms down. Place basket in a Dutch oven over

1 in. of water. Bring to a boil; cover and steam for 25-30 minutes or until cornmeal peels away from husk, adding water to pan as needed. Warm reserved pan juices; serve pan juices with tamales. Remove husks before eating. **Yield: 32 tamales.**

BEEF TOSTADAS

You can also use corn or flour tortillas to prepare these hearty specialties. To warm the tortillas, cook in a nonstick skillet for one minute on each side before layering with the fresh ingredients.

—Taste of Home Test Kitchen, Greendale, Wisconsin

1	pound lean ground beef
1	cup chopped sweet red pepper
1/2	cup chili sauce
1	teaspoon Mexican *or* taco seasoning
1/4	teaspoon salt
1/4	teaspoon pepper
1/2	cup sour cream
3	teaspoons chipotle sauce
6	tostada shells
3	cups shredded lettuce
1-1/2	cups guacamole
1-1/2	cups shredded Mexican cheese blend

In a large skillet, cook beef and red pepper over medium heat until meat is no longer pink; drain. Stir in the chili sauce, Mexican seasoning, salt and pepper; heat through.

In a small bowl, combine sour cream and chipotle sauce. Layer each tostada with the lettuce, meat mixture, guacamole, cheese and chipotle cream. **Yield: 6 servings.**

BEEF TOSTADAS

CHICKEN ENCHILADAS

CHICKEN ENCHILADAS

Leftover chicken is used to create a rich and creamy meal-in-one. This colorful dish has zippy flavor, and the use of chicken instead of beef is a pleasant surprise.

—Julie Moutray, Wichita, Kansas

1	can (16 ounces) refried beans
10	flour tortillas (8 inches), warmed
1	can (10-3/4 ounces) condensed cream of chicken soup, undiluted
1	cup (8 ounces) sour cream
3	to 4 cups cubed cooked chicken
3	cups (12 ounces) shredded cheddar cheese, *divided*
1	can (15 ounces) enchilada sauce
1/4	cup sliced green onions
1/4	cup sliced ripe olives

Shredded lettuce, optional

Spread about 2 tablespoons of beans on each tortilla. Combine soup and sour cream; stir in chicken. Spoon 1/3 to 1/2 cup down the center of each tortilla; top chicken filling with 1 tablespoon cheese.

Roll up and place enchiladas seam side down in a greased 13-in. x 9-in. baking dish. Pour enchilada sauce over top; sprinkle with the onions, olives and remaining cheese.

Bake, uncovered, at 350° for 35 minutes or until heated through. Just before serving, sprinkle lettuce around enchiladas if desired. **Yield: 10 servings.**

GRILLED SHRIMP FAJITAS

MEXICAN-STYLE PORK CHOPS

My family's fond of Mexican food, and I love to cook but not clean up. This easy one-pot meal makes everybody happy.

—Beverly Short, Gold Beach, Oregon

6	bone-in pork loin chops (1/2 inch thick and 8 ounces *each*)
2	tablespoons canola oil
1	medium onion, chopped
1	can (16 ounces) kidney beans, rinsed and drained
1	can (15-1/4 ounces) whole kernel corn, drained
1	can (10-3/4 ounces) condensed tomato soup, undiluted
1-1/4	cups water
1	cup uncooked instant rice
1/2	cup sliced ripe olives
2	to 3 teaspoons chili powder
1/2	teaspoon dried oregano
1/2	teaspoon salt
1/8	teaspoon pepper

In an ovenproof skillet, brown pork chops in oil on each side; remove and keep warm. In the same skillet, saute onion until tender. Stir in the remaining ingredients; bring to a boil.

Place chops over the onion mixture. Bake, uncovered, at 350° for 20-25 minutes or until meat juices run clear. **Yield: 6 servings.**

GRILLED SHRIMP FAJITAS

This entree assembles in very little time and without much preparation or cleanup. It's so delicious...and impressive enough to serve guests. My clan always shows up for this meal.

—Amy Hammons, Martinez, Georgia

1/2	pound sliced bacon
1/2	pound uncooked medium shrimp, peeled and deveined
1	medium green pepper, cut into 1-inch pieces
1	medium sweet red pepper, cut into 1-inch pieces
1	medium onion, cut into 1-inch pieces
1/2	cup barbecue sauce
6	flour tortillas (8 inches), warmed
1	cup shredded lettuce
1	medium tomato, diced
1/2	cup shredded cheddar cheese

In a large skillet, cook bacon over medium heat until cooked but not crisp. Drain bacon on paper towels. Wrap a strip of bacon around each shrimp; secure ends of bacon with toothpicks.

On six metal or soaked wooden skewers, alternately thread shrimp, peppers and onion. Grill, covered, over medium heat or broil 4 in. from the heat for 2-3 minutes on each side or until shrimp turn pink and vegetables are tender, basting frequently with barbecue sauce.

Remove shrimp and vegetables from skewers; discard toothpicks. Place on one side of each tortilla. Top with lettuce, tomato and cheese; fold over. **Yield: 6 servings.**

MEXICAN-STYLE PORK CHOPS

BEEF FLAUTAS

Zippy salsa verde is the dipping sauce of choice for these Southwestern delights. Created for two, this deep-fried Mexican dish became one of our favorites after our three daughters left the nest.

—Esther Danielson, San Marcos, California

SOFT CHICKEN TACOS

1/2	pound boneless beef chuck roast, cubed
2	tablespoons finely chopped onion
2	tablespoons canned chopped green chilies
1	garlic clove, minced
1/4	teaspoon ground cumin
1/4	teaspoon salt

Dash pepper
1-1/2 to 2 cups water
SALSA VERDE:

2	tomatillos, husks removed and rinsed, chopped
2	tablespoons finely chopped onion
1	teaspoon canola oil
2	teaspoons canned chopped green chilies
2	teaspoons minced fresh cilantro
4	garlic cloves, minced

Dash salt and pepper
2 flour tortillas (8 inches), warmed
Oil for frying

In a small saucepan, combine the first seven ingredients; add enough water just to cover. Bring the mixture to a boil. Reduce heat; cover and simmer for 55 minutes or until the meat is tender.

Meanwhile, in a small nonstick skillet, saute tomatillos and onion in oil until tender. Remove from the heat; stir in the chilies, cilantro, garlic, salt and pepper. Cool slightly. Process in a food processor or blender until pureed. Transfer the pureed mixture to a small bowl; cover and refrigerate until serving.

Remove meat from saucepan. Strain liquid, reserving onion mixture. When meat is cool enough to handle, shred with two forks. Combine onion mixture and meat; divide between tortillas. Roll up and secure with toothpicks.

In an electric skillet or deep-fat fryer, heat oil to 375°. Cook flautas until golden brown, turning to cook all sides. Drain flautas on paper towels and serve with salsa verde. **Yield: 2 servings.**

SOFT CHICKEN TACOS

I came up with this healthy chicken and bean filling for tacos since my husband needs to watch his cholesterol level. Sliced radishes make a unique crunchy topping.

—Ruth Peterson, Jenison, Michigan

1	pound boneless skinless chicken breasts, cut into 1 in. cubes
1	can (15 ounces) black beans, rinsed and drained
1	cup salsa
1	tablespoon taco seasoning
6	flour tortillas (8 inches), warmed

Toppings: Shredded lettuce, shredded reduced-fat cheddar cheese, sliced radishes, chopped tomatoes, sliced green onions and fat-free sour cream, optional

In a large skillet coated with cooking spray, cook chicken over medium heat until juices run clear. Stir in the beans, salsa and taco seasoning; heat through. Spoon the chicken mixture down the center of each tortilla; roll up. Serve with toppings of your choice. **Yield: 6 servings.**

Easy Kitchen Tips

When cutting chicken breasts, put your kitchen scissors to work to save time and make it easier on yourself.

Whenever a recipe calls for cubed chicken, simply use a pair of kitchen scissors instead of a knife.

BEEF-STUFFED SOPAIPILLAS

BEEF-STUFFED SOPAIPILLAS

When my brother and I were kids, we would visit a local restaurant for their wonderful Southwestern stuffed sopaipillas. This recipe takes me back to those delicious childhood memories. Even my Canadian husband raves about these!
—Lara Pennell, Irving, Texas

         2   cups all-purpose flour
         1   teaspoon salt
         1   teaspoon baking powder
       1/2   cup water
       1/4   cup evaporated milk
     1-1/2   teaspoons canola oil
Additional oil for frying
FILLING:
         1   pound ground beef
       3/4   cup chopped onion
       1/2   teaspoon salt
       1/2   teaspoon garlic powder
       1/4   teaspoon pepper
SAUCE:
         1   can (10-3/4 ounces) condensed cream of
             chicken soup, undiluted
       1/2   cup chicken broth
         1   can (4 ounces) chopped green chilies
       1/2   teaspoon onion powder
         2   cups (8 ounces) shredded cheddar cheese

In a large bowl, combine the flour, salt and baking powder. Stir in water, milk and oil with a fork until a ball forms. On a lightly floured surface, knead dough gently for 2-3 minutes. Cover and let stand for 15 minutes. Divide into four portions; roll each into a 6-1/2-in. circle.

In an electric skillet or deep-fat fryer, heat oil to 375°. Fry circles, one at a time, for 2-3 minutes on each side or until golden brown. Drain on paper towels.

In a large skillet, cook beef and onion until meat is no longer pink; drain. Stir in the salt, garlic powder and pepper. In a large saucepan, combine the soup, broth, chilies and onion powder; cook for 10 minutes or until heated through.

Cut a slit on one side of each sopaipilla; fill with 1/2 cup of meat mixture. Top with cheese. Serve with sauce. **Yield: 4 servings.**

FAJITA TORTILLA BOWLS

When brushed with butter and baked over custard cups, these spinach tortillas make crunchy bowls for crisp, fresh lettuce salads topped with savory pork and peppers.
—Katie Koziolek, Hartland, Minnesota

         6   spinach tortillas
         2   tablespoons butter, melted
         1   tablespoon canola oil
         1   pound boneless pork loin chops,
             cut into thin strips
         1   envelope fajita seasoning mix
         1   medium onion, thinly sliced
         1   sweet red pepper, thinly sliced
         1   green pepper, thinly sliced
     4-1/2   cups shredded lettuce
         1   medium tomato, chopped

Place six 10-oz. custard cups upside down in a shallow baking pan; set aside. Brush both sides of tortillas with butter; place in a single layer on ungreased baking sheets.

Bake, uncovered, at 425° for 1 minute. Place a tortilla over each custard cup, pinching sides to form a bowl shape. Bake for 7-8 minutes longer or until crisp. Remove tortilla from cups to cool on wire racks.

In a large skillet, combine pork and seasoning mix. Cook and stir over medium-high heat until meat juices run clear. Remove pork with a slotted spoon.

In the drippings, saute the onion and peppers until crisp-tender. Place the lettuce in tortilla bowls; top with the pork, pepper mixture and chopped tomato. **Yield: 6 servings.**

PORK CARNITAS

I use this recipe often when entertaining. I set out all the toppings, and folks have fun assembling their own carnitas. Because I am able to prepare everything ahead of time, I get to spend more time with my guests.

—Tracy Byers, Corvallis, Oregon

1   boneless pork shoulder *or* loin roast (2 to 3 pounds), trimmed and cut into 3-inch cubes
1/2 cup lime juice
1   teaspoon salt
1/2 teaspoon pepper
1/2 teaspoon crushed red pepper flakes
12 flour tortillas (6 inches), warmed
2   cups (8 ounces) shredded cheddar *or* Monterey Jack cheese
2   medium avocados, peeled and diced
2   medium tomatoes, diced
1   medium onion, diced

Shredded lettuce
Minced fresh cilantro, optional
Salsa

In a 3-qt. slow cooker, combine pork, lime juice, salt, pepper and pepper flakes. Cover and cook on high for 1 hour; stir. Reduce heat to low and cook 8-10 hours longer or until meat is very tender.

Shred pork with a fork (it may look somewhat pink). Spoon about 1/3 cup of filling down the center of each tortilla; top with cheese, avocados, tomatoes, onion, lettuce and cilantro if desired. Fold in bottom and sides of tortilla. Serve with salsa. **Yield: 12 servings.**

CHIPOTLE CHICKEN AND BEANS

I was skeptical about this recipe due to its combination of ingredients, but it became one of our all-time favorites.

—Jenny Kniesly, Dover, Ohio

3/4 cup water, *divided*
1/2 cup reduced-sodium chicken broth
1/2 cup uncooked long grain rice
6   boneless skinless chicken breast halves (4 ounces *each*)
1/4 teaspoon salt
3   bacon strips, diced
1   cup chopped onion
3   garlic cloves, minced
1   cup chopped plum tomatoes
1/2 teaspoon ground cumin
1/4 teaspoon ground cinnamon
1/2 cup whole-berry cranberry sauce
4-1/2 teaspoons minced chipotle peppers in adobo sauce
1-1/2 teaspoons lime juice
1   can (15 ounces) black beans, rinsed and drained
1   can (15 ounces) white kidney *or* cannellini beans, rinsed and drained

In a small saucepan, bring 1/2 cup water and broth to a boil. Stir in rice. Reduce heat; cover and simmer for 15-18 minutes or until rice is tender.

Meanwhile, cut each chicken breast half widthwise into six strips. Sprinkle with salt. In a large nonstick skillet coated with cooking spray, cook chicken for 5 minutes on each side or until lightly browned. Remove chicken strips and keep warm.

In the same skillet, cook bacon over medium heat until crisp. Using a slotted spoon, remove to paper towels. Drain, reserving 1/2 teaspoon drippings. In the drippings, saute onion and garlic until tender. Add the tomatoes, cumin and cinnamon; cook for 2 minutes. Stir in the cranberry sauce, chipotle peppers, lime juice and remaining water. Bring to a boil.

Return chicken to the pan. Reduce heat; cover and simmer for 6-10 minutes or until chicken juices run clear. Remove and keep warm. Add rice and beans to the skillet; heat through. Serve chicken over bean mixture; sprinkle with bacon. **Yield: 6 servings.**

CHIPOTLE CHICKEN AND BEANS

Southwestern Specialties

SANTA FE CHICKEN, P. 78

SOUTHWEST STUFFED CHICKEN

SOUTHWEST STUFFED CHICKEN

Our daughter served these tender chicken rolls to us a long time ago, and we've enjoyed them often since then. A zippy cheese filling gives them special flavor while a seasoned, golden coating enhances their lovely appearance.

—Alcy Thorne, Los Molinos, California

  6   boneless skinless chicken breast halves
      (4 ounces *each*)
  6   ounces Monterey Jack cheese, cut into 2-inch x
      1/2-inch sticks
  2   cans (4 ounces *each*) chopped green chilies,
      drained
1/2   cup dry bread crumbs
1/4   cup grated Parmesan cheese
  1   tablespoon chili powder
1/2   teaspoon salt
1/4   teaspoon ground cumin
3/4   cup all-purpose flour
1/2   cup butter, melted

Flatten chicken to 1/8-in. thickness. Place a cheese stick down the middle of each; top with chilies. Roll up and tuck in ends. Secure with a toothpick.

In a shallow bowl, combine the bread crumbs, Parmesan cheese, chili powder, salt and cumin. Place flour in another shallow bowl. Place butter in a third shallow bowl. Coat chicken with flour, then dip in butter and roll in crumb mixture.

Place the chicken roll-ups, seam side down, in a greased 13-in. x 9-in. baking dish. Bake, uncovered, at 400° for 25 minutes or until chicken juices run clear. Discard the toothpicks. **Yield: 6 servings.**

TAMALE PIE

When time is tight on weekdays, I can always count on this zesty, deep-dish pie. It satisfies my family's taste for Mexican food and keeps us on schedule.

—Nancy Roberts, Cave City, Arkansas

  1   pound ground beef
1/4   pound bulk pork sausage
1/4   cup chopped onion
  1   garlic clove, minced
  1   can (14-1/2 ounces) stewed tomatoes, drained
  1   can (11 ounces) whole kernel corn, drained
  1   can (6 ounces) tomato paste
1/4   cup sliced ripe olives
1-1/2 teaspoons chili powder
1/2   teaspoon salt
  1   egg
1/3   cup milk
  1   package (8-1/2 ounces) corn bread/muffin mix
Dash paprika
1/2   cup shredded cheddar cheese

In a 2-1/2-qt. microwave-safe dish, combine the beef, sausage, onion and garlic. Cover and microwave on high for 4-5 minutes, stirring once to crumble meat. Drain. Add the tomatoes, corn, tomato paste, olives, chili powder and salt; mix well. Cover and microwave on high for 4-6 minutes or until heated through.

In a large bowl, beat egg; add milk and corn bread mix. Stir just until moistened. Spoon over meat mixture; sprinkle with paprika.

Microwave, uncovered, on high for 7-8 minutes or until a toothpick inserted near the center of the corn bread comes out clean. Sprinkle with cheese. **Yield: 6 servings.**

Editor's Note: This recipe was tested in a 1,100-watt microwave.

TAMALE PIE

TACO-FILLED PASTA SHELLS

TACO-FILLED PASTA SHELLS

I've been stuffing pasta shells with different fillings for years, but my family enjoys this version with taco-seasoned meat the most. The shells freeze very well, making them a convenient meal on busy nights. Simply take out only the number of shells you need, add the zippy taco sauce and bake.

—Marge Hodel, Roanoke, Illinois

2   pounds ground beef
2   envelopes taco seasoning
1   package (8 ounces) cream cheese, cubed
24   uncooked jumbo pasta shells
1/4   cup butter, melted
ADDITIONAL INGREDIENTS (for each casserole):
1   cup salsa
1   cup taco sauce
1   cup (4 ounces) shredded cheddar cheese
1   cup (4 ounces) shredded Monterey Jack cheese
1-1/2   cups crushed tortilla chips
1   cup (8 ounces) sour cream
3   green onions, chopped

In a Dutch oven, cook ground beef over medium heat until no longer pink; drain. Add taco seasoning; prepare according to package directions. Add cream cheese; cook and stir for 5-10 minutes or until melted. Transfer meat mixture to a bowl; chill for 1 hour.

Cook pasta shells according to package directions; drain. Gently toss with butter. Fill each pasta shell with about 3 tablespoons of meat mixture. Place 12 shells in a freezer container. Cover and freeze for up to 3 months.

To prepare remaining shells, spoon salsa into a greased 9-in. square baking dish. Top with stuffed shells and taco sauce. Cover and bake at 350° for 30 minutes. Uncover; sprinkle with cheeses and crushed tortilla chips. Bake 15 minutes longer or until heated through. Serve with sour cream and onions.

To use frozen shells: Thaw in refrigerator for 24 hours (shells will be partially frozen). Spoon salsa into a greased 9-in. square baking dish; top with shells and taco sauce. Cover; bake at 350° for 40 minutes. Uncover; continue as directed above. **Yield: 2 casseroles (6 servings each).**

SOUTHWESTERN DEEP-DISH PIZZA

With a rich, hearty beef and bean filling, a slice of this slightly spicy pizza goes a long way. I enjoy experimenting with my cooking and have studied ethnic cuisine all over the world.

—Diane Halferty, Tucson, Arizona

2-1/2   cups biscuit/baking mix
1/2   cup cornmeal
3/4   cup water
1   pound ground beef
1   medium onion, diced
1   can (8 ounces) tomato sauce
2   teaspoons chili powder
1   teaspoon ground cinnamon
1   can (16 ounces) refried beans
Hot pepper sauce to taste
2   cups (8 ounces) shredded Monterey Jack *or* cheddar cheese
Salsa and sliced ripe olives, optional

In a large bowl, combine biscuit mix and cornmeal. Stir in the water until mixture forms a soft dough. Press the dough onto the bottom and up the sides of a lightly greased 15-in. x 10-in. baking pan. Bake at 425° for 10 minutes or until crust is lightly browned.

Meanwhile, in a large skillet, cook beef and onion over medium heat until meat is no longer pink; drain. Add the tomato sauce, chili powder and cinnamon. Bring to a boil. Reduce heat; simmer, uncovered, for 5 minutes. Remove from the heat.

Combine refried beans and hot pepper sauce; spread over crust. Top with meat mixture; sprinkle with cheese. Bake at 425° for 10 minutes or until cheese is melted. Let stand 10 minutes before cutting. Serve with salsa and olives if desired. **Yield: 16 servings.**

ARIZONA CHICKEN

I have a large collection of Southwest-inspired recipes. Served with either pasta or rice, this is one of my husband's favorites. The moist, flavorful chicken suits any occasion, plus it can be prepared to serve any number of guests.

—Carolyn Deming, Miami, Arizona

6 boneless skinless chicken breast halves
(4 ounces *each*)
1/4 cup canola oil, *divided*
1 medium onion, sliced
4 cups chopped fresh tomatoes
2 celery ribs, sliced
1/4 cup water
1/4 cup sliced pimiento-stuffed olives
2 teaspoons garlic powder
2 teaspoons dried oregano
1 teaspoon salt, optional
1/4 teaspoon pepper
1/2 pound fresh mushrooms, sliced

In a skillet, brown chicken on both sides in 2 tablespoons of oil. Remove and set aside. In the same skillet, saute onion in remaining oil until tender. Add the tomatoes, celery, water, olives, garlic powder, oregano, salt if desired and pepper; bring to a boil.

Cover and simmer for 15 minutes. Return chicken to pan. Simmer, uncovered, for 15 minutes. Add mushrooms; simmer 15 minutes longer or until chicken juices run clear. **Yield: 6 servings.**

ARIZONA CHICKEN

MOM'S PAELLA

MOM'S PAELLA

I enjoy cooking various regional dishes, especially those that call for lots of rice. Like my mom, I often prepare this dish when hosting a special Sunday get-together.

—Ena Quiggle, Goodhue, Minnesota

1-1/2 cups cubed cooked chicken
1 cup cubed fully cooked ham
1/2 cup sliced fully cooked smoked sausage
(1/4-inch slices)
1 medium onion, chopped
1 small green pepper, chopped
4 tablespoons olive oil, *divided*
1/4 cup pimiento-stuffed olives, halved
1/2 cup raisins, optional
1 cup uncooked converted rice
2 garlic cloves, minced
3 teaspoons ground turmeric
1-1/2 teaspoons curry powder
2-1/4 cups chicken broth
1-1/2 cups frozen mixed vegetables

In a large skillet, saute the chicken, ham, sausage, onion and green pepper in 2 tablespoons oil for 3-5 minutes or until onion is tender. Add olives and raisins if desired. Cook 2-3 minutes longer or until heated through, stirring occasionally; remove meat and vegetable mixture from pan and keep warm.

In the same skillet, saute rice in remaining oil for 2-3 minutes or until lightly browned. Stir in the garlic, turmeric and curry. Return meat and vegetables to pan; toss lightly. Add broth and mixed vegetables; bring to a boil. Reduce heat; cover and simmer for 25-30 minutes or until rice is tender. **Yield: 6-8 servings.**

SANTA FE CHICKEN

SANTA FE CHICKEN

My day is busy from the time I wake up until I go to bed. So this quick and meaty main dish is one of my menu mainstays. With its lovely golden color, it's pretty enough to serve to company or as a special dinner.

—Debra Cook, Pampa, Texas

- 1 large onion, chopped
- 1 tablespoon butter
- 1-1/4 cups chicken broth
- 1 cup salsa
- 1 cup uncooked long grain rice
- 1/8 teaspoon garlic powder
- 4 boneless skinless chicken breast halves (4 ounces *each*)
- 3/4 cup shredded cheddar cheese

Chopped fresh cilantro, optional

In a large skillet, saute onion in butter until tender. Add chicken broth and salsa; bring to a boil. Stir in rice and garlic powder. Place chicken over the rice; cover and simmer for 10 minutes.

Turn chicken; cook 10-15 minutes longer or until a meat thermometer reaches 170°. Remove from the heat. Sprinkle with cheese; cover and let stand for 5 minutes. Garnish with cilantro if desired. **Yield: 4 servings.**

MEATY CORN BREAD SQUARES

Working full-time outside of the home doesn't allow me to cook as often as I'd like. So when I get a spare moment, I enjoy experimenting in the kitchen. These tasty squares are an all-time favorite creation of mine.

—Rebecca Meyerkorth, Wamego, Kansas

- 1 can (10 ounces) diced tomatoes with green chilies, undrained
- 1 pound diced fully cooked ham
- 1/4 cup chopped onion
- 2 teaspoons chili powder
- 1 garlic clove, minced
- 1 tablespoon cornstarch
- 1 cup all-purpose flour
- 1/2 cup cornmeal
- 2 teaspoons baking powder
- 2 eggs
- 1 can (16 ounces) whole kernel corn, drained
- 3/4 cup milk
- 3 tablespoons canola oil
- 1-1/2 cups (6 ounces) shredded Monterey Jack cheese

Salsa, optional

Drain tomatoes, reserving juice; set tomatoes aside. In a large skillet, combine the ham, onion, chili powder, garlic and tomatoes. Cook over medium heat until onion is crisp-tender. Combine the cornstarch and reserved juice. Gradually add to meat mixture. Bring to a boil over medium heat. Reduce heat; cook and stir for 2 minutes or until thickened. Set aside.

In a large bowl, combine flour, cornmeal and baking powder. In another bowl, combine the eggs, corn, milk and oil; stir into dry ingredients just until moistened. Spread half the batter into a greased 9-in. square baking dish. Spoon meat mixture over batter. Sprinkle with cheese. Spoon remaining batter on top.

Bake, uncovered, at 350° for 35-40 minutes or until golden brown. Let stand for 5 minutes before cutting. Serve with salsa if desired. **Yield: 6 servings.**

MEATY CORN BREAD SQUARES

FIESTA CORNMEAL PIZZA

FIESTA CORNMEAL PIZZA

You'll love the cornmeal crust of this "knife-and-fork" pizza that has been popular with my family for years. It's a nice change from traditional pizza and so simple to make.

—Mirien Church, Aurora, Colorado

1 cup cornmeal
1-1/3 cups water, *divided*
6 tablespoons grated Parmesan cheese, *divided*
1 medium onion, chopped
1 small green pepper, julienned
1 garlic clove, minced
2 tablespoons olive oil
1 can (8 ounces) tomato sauce
8 fresh mushrooms, sliced
3/4 teaspoon dried basil
3/4 teaspoon dried oregano
1/4 teaspoon pepper
1 can (15 ounces) black beans, rinsed and drained
1-1/2 cups (6 ounces) shredded part-skim mozzarella cheese, *divided*
1/2 cup sliced ripe olives

In a small bowl, combine the cornmeal and 2/3 cup water. In a large saucepan, bring the remaining water to a boil. Gradually whisk in the cornmeal mixture; cook and stir until thickened. Stir in 2 tablespoons Parmesan cheese. When cool enough to handle, pat into a greased 12-in. pizza pan. Bake at 375° for 15 minutes or until lightly browned. Cool slightly.

Meanwhile, in a large skillet, saute the onion, green pepper and garlic in oil until tender. Add the tomato sauce, mushrooms, basil, oregano and pepper. Cover and cook for 5 minutes. Add the beans.

Sprinkle 1/2 cup mozzarella and 2 tablespoons Parmesan cheese over crust. Top cheese with the bean mixture and remaining cheeses. Sprinkle with olives. Bake pizza at 375° for 15-20 minutes or until cheese is melted. **Yield: 4-6 servings.**

TACO MUFFINS

I'm always inventing new recipes. This is one that went over very well with family and friends. The mouth-watering muffins are excellent when accompanied by refried beans.

—Donna Krivdo, Prescot Valley, Arizona

1 pound ground beef
3/4 cup water
1 envelope taco seasoning
1/4 cup butter, softened
1/4 cup sugar
1 egg
1-3/4 cups all-purpose flour
4 teaspoons baking powder
1/4 teaspoon baking soda
1/4 teaspoon salt
1 cup buttermilk
1 cup salsa
1 cup (4 ounces) shredded cheddar cheese

In a large skillet, cook beef over medium heat until no longer pink; drain. Add water and taco seasoning; simmer, uncovered, for 15 minutes. Cool.

In a large bowl, cream butter and sugar until light and fluffy. Beat in egg. Combine dry ingredients; add to the creamed mixture alternately with buttermilk, beating well after each addition. Fold in meat mixture.

Fill greased muffin cups two-thirds full. Bake at 425° for 12-15 minutes or until golden brown. Carefully remove muffins to a greased 13-in. x 9-in. baking dish. Top each with salsa and cheese. Bake 5 minutes longer or until the cheese is melted. **Yield: about 16 muffins.**

Editor's Note: To serve Taco Muffins as an appetizer, bake in miniature muffin cups, reducing the baking time, and have your guests top their own servings with salsa and cheese.

ARIZONA CORN BREAD

ARIZONA CORN BREAD

Spicy jalapeno and pepper Jack cheese jazz up ordinary corn bread. Sour cream keeps each golden slice deliciously moist.
—Margaret Pache, Mesa, Arizona

1	cup cornmeal
2	tablespoons sugar
2	packages (1/4 ounce *each*) active dry yeast
1	teaspoon salt
1/2	teaspoon baking soda
1/4	teaspoon pepper
1	cup (8 ounces) sour cream
1/2	cup canola oil
1/2	cup chopped green onions
2	eggs
1-1/4	cups shredded pepper Jack cheese
1	cup cream-style corn
2	jalapeno peppers, seeded and chopped
5	to 6 cups all-purpose flour

Additional cornmeal
Melted butter

In a large bowl, combine the first six ingredients; set aside. In a saucepan, heat the sour cream, oil and onions to 120°-130°. Add to cornmeal mixture; bet until blended. Beat in eggs, cheese, corn and jalapeno. Stir in enough flour to form a stiff dough.

Turn onto a floured surface; knead until smooth and elastic, about 6-8 minutes. Place in a greased bowl, turning once to grease top. Cover and let rise in a warm place until doubled, about 1 hour.

Punch dough down. Turn onto a lightly floured surface; divide in half. Shape into two loaves. Grease two 9-in. x 5-in. loaf pans; dust with additional cornmeal. Place

loaves seam side down in prepared pans. Cover and let rise until doubled, about 30 minutes.

Brush butter over loaves. Bake at 375° for 30-35 minutes or until golden brown; cover loosely with foil if top browns too quickly. Remove from pans to wire racks to cool. **Yield: 2 loaves (16 slices each).**

Editor's Note: *When cutting hot peppers, disposable gloves are recommended. Avoid touching your face.*

SOUTHWESTERN HASH

I had a similar dish at a restaurant in Arizona and enjoyed it so much I re-created it at home. It's a special way to serve eggs and perfect for breakfast, lunch or dinner.
—Marilyn Paradis, Woodburn, Oregon

8	bacon strips, diced
1/2	cup chopped onion
1	garlic clove, minced
4	cups frozen cubed hash brown potatoes
1	can (4 ounces) chopped green chilies
1	medium tomato, diced
4	eggs, poached

Salsa

In a large skillet, cook bacon over medium heat until crisp. Using a slotted spoon, remove to paper towels; drain, reserving 2 tablespoons drippings. Set bacon aside.

In the same skillet, saute onion and garlic in reserved drippings until tender. Stir in hash browns and chilies. Cook and stir over low heat for 20 minutes or until lightly browned and heated through.

Just before serving, add tomato. Spoon onto plates; top with eggs and bacon. Serve with salsa. **Yield: 4 servings.**

SOUTHWESTERN HASH

FLOUR TORTILLA MIX

I love this recipe for homemade flour and spinach tortillas. I make a batch, then use them whenever a recipe calls for the packaged variety to lend the meal more authenticity.

—Katie Koziolek, Hartland, Minnesota

8-1/2 cups all-purpose flour
 2/3 cup nonfat dry milk powder
   1 tablespoon baking powder
   1 teaspoon salt
   1 cup shortening
ADDITIONAL INGREDIENTS FOR FLOUR TORTILLAS:
 1/2 cup plus 1 to 2 tablespoons water
ADDITIONAL INGREDIENTS FOR SPINACH TORTILLAS:
 1/4 cup frozen chopped spinach, thawed and
       squeezed dry
 1/3 cup plus 2 to 3 tablespoons water

In a large bowl, combine the flour, milk powder, baking powder and salt. Cut in shortening until crumbly. Store in an airtight container in a cool dry place for up to 6 months. **Yield: 4 batches (about 10 cups total).**

To prepare flour tortillas: In a large bowl, combine 2-1/2 cups tortilla mix and 1/2 cup water. Stir with a fork until mixture forms a ball, adding additional water if necessary.

Turn onto a lightly floured surface; knead 6-8 times or until smooth and combined. Divide into 10 portions. Roll each piece into an 8-in. circle.

In a 10-in. ungreased nonstick skillet, cook each tortilla over medium-high heat for 30-45 seconds or until bubbles form. Turn tortilla, pressing bubbles down with a spatula. Cook about 30 seconds longer or until lightly browned. **Yield: 10 tortillas (8 inches each).**

To prepare spinach tortillas: In a blender, combine spinach and 1/3 cup water; cover and process until smooth. In a large bowl, combine 2-1/2 cups tortilla mix and spinach mixture. Continue as directed for flour tortillas. **Yield: 10 tortillas (8 inches each).**

SOUTHWEST VEGETARIAN BAKE

Creamy and comforting, this spicy meatless casserole hits the spot on chilly nights. But I've found it's great any time I have a taste for Mexican food with all the fixings.

—Patricia Gale, Monticello, Illinois

SOUTHWEST VEGETARIAN BAKE

 3/4 cup uncooked brown rice
1-1/2 cups water
   1 can (15 ounces) black beans, rinsed and
       drained
   1 can (11 ounces) Mexicorn, drained
   1 can (10 ounces) diced tomatoes and green
       chilies
   1 cup salsa
   1 cup (8 ounces) sour cream
   1 cup (4 ounces) shredded cheddar cheese
 1/4 teaspoon pepper
 1/2 cup chopped red onion
   1 can (2-1/4 ounces) sliced ripe olives, drained
   1 cup (4 ounces) shredded reduced-fat Mexican
       cheese blend

In a large saucepan, bring rice and water to a boil. Reduce heat; cover and simmer for 35-40 minutes or until rice is tender.

In a large bowl, combine the beans, Mexicorn, tomatoes, salsa, sour cream, cheddar cheese, pepper and rice. Transfer to a shallow 2-1/2-qt. baking dish coated with cooking spray. Sprinkle with onion and olives.

Bake, uncovered, at 350° for 30 minutes. Sprinkle with Mexican cheese. Bake 5-10 minutes longer or until heated through and cheese is melted. Let stand for 10 minutes before serving. **Yield: 8 servings.**

TACO BRAID

TACO BRAID

This pretty braided sandwich is a real winner! My daughter entered the recipe in a state 4-H beef cooking contest and won a trip to the national competition. Everyone who tastes it comments on its lovely appearance and savory filling.
—Lucile Proctor, Panguitch, Utah

1	teaspoon active dry yeast
2	tablespoons sugar, *divided*
3/4	cup warm water (110° to 115°), *divided*
2	tablespoons butter, softened
2	tablespoons nonfat dry milk powder
1	egg, lightly beaten
1/2	teaspoon salt
2	cups all-purpose flour

FILLING:

1	pound lean ground beef
1/4	cup sliced fresh mushrooms
1	can (8 ounces) tomato sauce
2	tablespoons taco seasoning
1	egg, lightly beaten
1/2	cup shredded cheddar cheese
1/4	cup sliced ripe olives

In a large mixing bowl, dissolve yeast and 1 teaspoon sugar in 1/2 cup water; let stand for 5 minutes. Add the butter, milk powder, egg, salt and remaining sugar and water. Stir in enough flour to form a soft dough.

Turn the dough onto a floured surface; knead until smooth and elastic, about 6-8 minutes. Place the dough in a greased bowl, turning once to greased top. Cover dough and let rise in a warm place until doubled in size, about 1 hour.

In a large skillet, cook the ground beef and mushrooms over medium heat until meat is no longer pink; drain. Stir in the tomato sauce and the taco seasoning. Set aside 1 tablespoon beaten egg. Stir remaining egg into the beef mixture. Cool beef mixture completely.

Punch dough down. Turn onto a lightly floured surface; roll into a 15-in. x 12-in. rectangle. Place on a greased baking sheet. Spread filling lengthwise down center third of rectangle. Sprinkle with cheese and olives.

On each long side, cut 1-in.-wide strips about 2-1/2 in. into center. Starting at one end, fold alternating strips at an angle across filling. Pinch ends to seal and tuck under. Cover and let rise for 30 minutes.

Brush with reserved egg. Bake at 350° for 20-25 minutes or until golden brown. Remove from pan to a wire rack to cool. **Yield: 12-16 servings.**

BACON-POTATO BURRITOS

I've been cooking for years. To keep my interest, I like to try new recipes like these unique breakfast burritos.
—Reesa Byrd, Enterprise, Alabama

8	bacon strips
1-1/2	cups frozen Southern-style hash brown potatoes
2	teaspoons minced dried onion
4	eggs
1/4	cup milk
1	teaspoon Worcestershire sauce
1/4	teaspoon salt
1/4	teaspoon pepper
1	cup (4 ounces) shredded cheddar cheese
6	flour tortillas (8 inches)

In a large skillet, cook bacon until crisp. Drain on paper towels; set aside.

Brown potatoes and onion in drippings. In a bowl, beat eggs; add milk, Worcestershire sauce, salt and pepper. Pour over potatoes; cook and stir until eggs are set. Crumble bacon and stir into eggs. Sprinkle with cheese.

Meanwhile, warm the tortillas according to package directions. Spoon the egg mixture down center of tortillas; fold in sides of tortilla. Serve the burritos with salsa. **Yield: 4-6 servings.**

FAJITA FRITTATA

FAJITA FRITTATA

This is a super-flavorful and speedy entree ideal for breakfast or lunch. It takes me just a few minutes to prepare. However, whenever I ask my family what they want for dinner, this seems to be their most popular request. I don't mind, as it takes just a few minutes to prepare.

—Mary Ann Gomez, Lombard, Illinois

- 1/2 pound boneless skinless chicken breast, cut into strips
- 1 small onion, cut into thin strips
- 1/2 medium green pepper, cut into thin strips
- 1 teaspoon lime juice
- 1/2 teaspoon salt
- 1/2 teaspoon ground cumin
- 1/2 teaspoon chili powder
- 2 tablespoons canola oil
- 8 eggs, lightly beaten
- 1 cup (4 ounces) shredded Colby-Monterey Jack cheese

Salsa and sour cream, optional

In a large ovenproof skillet, saute the chicken, onion, green pepper, lime juice, salt, cumin and chili powder in oil until chicken juices run clear.

Pour eggs over chicken mixture. Cover and cook over medium-low heat for 8-10 minutes or until eggs are nearly set. Uncover; broil 6 in. from the heat for 2-3 minutes or until eggs are set. Sprinkle with cheese. Cover and let stand for 1 minute or until cheese is melted. Serve with salsa and sour cream if desired. **Yield: 8 servings.**

PEPPER JACK BATTER BREAD

This flavorful loaf is flecked with green chilies. A thick slice of this moist and slightly spicy bread is hearty enough to turn a steaming bowl of soup into a complete meal.

—Becky Asher, Keizer, Oregon

- 1 package (1/4 ounce) active dry yeast
- 1/4 cup warm water (110° to 115°)
- 1/2 cup warm milk (110° to 115°)
- 1/3 cup butter, melted
- 2 tablespoons sugar
- 1 teaspoon salt
- 2 eggs
- 2-1/4 to 2-3/4 cups all-purpose flour
- 1/2 cup plus 5 teaspoons cornmeal, *divided*
- 1 can (4 ounces) chopped green chilies, drained
- 4 ounces pepper Jack cheese, shredded

In a large bowl, dissolve yeast in warm water. Add the milk, butter, sugar, salt, eggs and 1 cup flour. Beat on low speed for 30 seconds. Beat on medium for 2 minutes. Stir in 1/2 cup cornmeal and remaining flour. Stir in chilies and cheese. Do not knead. Cover and let rise in a warm place until doubled, about 45 minutes.

Stir dough down. Sprinkle 3 teaspoons cornmeal into a greased 9-in. x 5-in. loaf pan. Spoon batter into pan. Sprinkle with remaining cornmeal. Cover and let rise in a warm place until doubled, about 30 minutes.

Bake at 375° for 45-50 minutes or until bread sounds hollow when tapped. Cool bread for 10 minutes before removing loaf from pan to a wire rack. Store in the refrigerator. **Yield: 1 loaf (16 slices).**

Easy Kitchen Tips

When mixing bread dough, it is best to use a plastic bowl instead of a glass one. Using a plastic bowl prevents the bread dough from sticking to the sides of the bowl and makes the dough much easier to handle.

After the bread is baked, prevent the loaves from drying out and going to waste by sealing them in large plastic freezer bags. You can then freeze the loaves for up to 3 months.

You can also slice the loaves before freezing. Doing this allows you to pull out a few slices of bread at a time instead of thawing the entire loaf.

MEXICAN MEAT LOAF

MEXICAN MEAT LOAF

I love to experiment with all kinds of recipes. A dash of chili powder gives this meat loaf fun Mexican flavor that's complemented by zesty picante sauce poured over the top.

—Debra Jane Webb, Muskogee, Oklahoma

3/4 cup milk
2 eggs, lightly beaten
1/2 cup dry bread crumbs
1/4 cup finely chopped onion
1/2 teaspoon salt
1/2 teaspoon pepper
1/2 teaspoon chili powder
1-1/2 pounds lean ground beef
1 jar (16 ounces) picante sauce

In a large bowl, combine the first seven ingredients. Add beef and mix well. Pat into a greased 8-in. x 4-in. loaf pan.

Bake, uncovered, at 350° for 1 hour or until a meat thermometer reaches 160°. Top with warm picante sauce. **Yield: 6 servings.**

GREEN CHILI 'N' RICE CASSEROLE

This recipe is a three-way winner. It is inexpensive, takes only minutes to prepare and tastes fantastic. It is also an excellent way to use up leftover cooked rice.

—Marilyn Scroggs, Lees Summit, Missouri

3 cups cooked long grain rice
1-1/2 cups (6 ounces) shredded cheddar cheese
1-1/2 cups (12 ounces) 4% cottage cheese
1 cans (4 ounces) chopped green chilies, drained
1/3 cup milk

1/3 cup chopped roasted red peppers
1 can (8-3/4 ounces) whole kernel corn, drained
1/4 cup grated Parmesan cheese

In a greased 2-qt. baking dish, combine the first seven ingredients. Sprinkle with Parmesan cheese. Cover and bake at 350° for 30-35 minutes or until heated through. **Yield: 6-8 servings.**

NACHO PIE

Crunchy nacho-flavored chips create the yummy crust in this kid-pleasing main dish. The hearty filling features simple ingredients that I usually have on hand, including ground beef, chili beans and mozzarella cheese.

—LaVerna Mjones, Moorhead, Minnesota

4 cups nacho tortilla chips, coarsely crushed
1 pound ground beef
1/2 cup chopped onion
Salt and pepper to taste
1 can (15-1/2 ounces) chili beans
1 can (8 ounces) tomato sauce
1 cup (4 ounces) shredded part-skim mozzarella cheese

Place chips in a lightly greased 9-in. pie plate and set aside. In a large skillet over medium heat, cook beef and onion until meat is no longer pink; drain. Sprinkle with salt and pepper. Spoon over chips. Top with beans, tomato sauce and cheese.

Bake, uncovered, at 375° for 15-17 minutes or until heated through and cheese is melted. **Yield: 4-6 servings.**

NACHO PIE

TEX-MEX BISCUITS

TEX-MEX BISCUITS

I love cooking with green chilies because they add so much spark to ordinary dishes. Once while making a pot of chili, I had some green chilies left over and mixed them into my biscuit dough, creating this recipe. The fresh-from-the-oven treats are a wonderful accompaniment to chili or soup.

—Angie Trolz, Jackson, Michigan

      2   cups biscuit/baking mix
    2/3   cup milk
      1   cup (4 ounces) finely shredded cheddar cheese
      1   can (4 ounces) chopped green chilies, drained

In a large bowl, combine biscuit mix and milk until a soft dough forms. Stir in cheese and chilies. Turn dough onto a floured surface; knead 10 times. Roll dough out to 1/2-in. thickness; cut with a 2-1/2-in. biscuit cutter.

Place on an ungreased baking sheet. Bake at 450° for 8-10 minutes or until biscuits are golden brown. Serve warm. **Yield: about 1 dozen.**

SALSA SAUSAGE QUICHE

A prepared pastry crust hurries along the assembly of this hearty morning dish. Served with sour cream and additional salsa, it's a breakfast and brunch favorite. If you're feeding a crowd, make two—they disappear fast!

—Dorothy Sorensen, Naples, Florida

    3/4   pound bulk pork sausage
      1   unbaked pastry shell (9 inches)
      2   cups (8 ounces) shredded cheddar cheese, *divided*
      3   eggs
      1   cup salsa

Crumble sausage into a large skillet. Cook over medium heat until no longer pink; drain. Transfer to the pastry shell. Sprinkle with half of the cheese. In a small bowl, lightly beat the eggs; stir in salsa. Pour over cheese.

Bake at 375° for 30-35 minutes or until knife inserted near the center comes out clean. Sprinkle with the remaining cheese. Bake 5 minutes longer or until the cheese is melted. **Yield: 8 servings.**

CHICKEN FAJITA PIZZA

For a no-fuss dinner, I can always count on this zippy, fajita-style pizza. I keep cooked diced chicken in my freezer to streamline the prep time even more.

—Charmaine Potter, Mission Viejo, California

    1/3   cup julienned green pepper
    1/4   teaspoon chili powder
    1/8   teaspoon minced garlic
Dash salt
      1   teaspoon olive oil
    2/3   cup diced cooked chicken
      1   prebaked mini Italian bread shell crust (8 inches)
    1/4   cup salsa
    1/3   cup shredded Monterey Jack cheese

In a large skillet, cook the green pepper, chili powder, garlic and salt in oil over medium heat for 3-4 minutes or until pepper is crisp-tender. Add chicken; heat through.

Spoon onto pizza crust; top with salsa and cheese. Place on a baking sheet. Bake at 425° for 10-15 minutes or until cheese is melted. **Yield: 2 servings.**

CHICKEN FAJITA PIZZA

MEXICAN OMELET

MEXICAN OMELET

Hearty enough for brunch, lunch or even dinner, this tasty omelet from our Test Kitchen boasts tangy Southwest appeal.

—Taste of Home Test Kitchen, Greendale, Wisconsin

- 1/2 cup chopped peeled ripe avocado
- 2 tablespoons sour cream
- 2 tablespoons chopped green chilies
- 1 tablespoon chopped onion
- 1/2 teaspoon lemon juice
- 1/4 teaspoon salt, optional
- 1/4 teaspoon pepper

Dash hot pepper sauce
- 2 tablespoons butter
- 1 corn tortilla (6 inches), cut into 1/2-inch pieces
- 4 eggs
- 1/2 cup shredded Monterey Jack cheese

Salsa, optional

In a small bowl, combine the avocado, sour cream, chilies, onion, lemon juice, salt if desired, pepper and hot pepper sauce; set aside.

In a 10-in. nonstick skillet, melt butter over medium-high heat. Add tortilla pieces; cook for 2 minutes or until softened. Meanwhile, whisk eggs. Add eggs to skillet (mixture should set immediately at edges).

As eggs set, push cooked edges toward the center, letting uncooked portion flow underneath. When the eggs are set, spoon avocado mixture over one side and sprinkle with cheese; fold other side over filling.

Invert omelet onto a plate. Cover and let stand for 1-1/2 minutes or until cheese is melted. Serve with salsa if desired. **Yield: 2 servings.**

TACO CRESCENTS

These quick-to-fix pockets hold a yummy taco-flavored filling that kids gobble up. Moms like me appreciate that they are so simple to make and freeze well, too.

—Eleanor Lapen, Chicago, Illinois

- 3/4 pound ground beef
- 1/4 cup chopped onion
- 1 package (1-1/4 ounces) taco seasoning
- 1 can (4-1/4 ounces) chopped ripe olives, drained
- 2 eggs, lightly beaten
- 1/2 cup shredded cheddar cheese
- 2 tubes (8 ounces) tubes refrigerated crescent rolls

In a large skillet, cook beef and onion until meat is no longer pink; drain. Stir in taco seasoning and olives; set aside to cool. Stir in eggs and cheese.

Unroll crescent roll dough and separate into triangles. Place the triangles on an ungreased baking sheet. Place 2 tablespoons meat mixture onto each triangle. Roll and shape into crescents. Bake at 375° for 10-15 minutes or until lightly browned. **Yield: 8 servings.**

SOUTHWEST STUFFED PEPPERS

Looking for a great way to give leftover meat loaf a whole new taste? Try this simple stuffed-peppers variation. The tasty filling in these tender pepper cups gets its zip from salsa and cumin.

—Greg Greinke, Round Rock, Texas

- 4 medium green *or* sweet red peppers
- 1/2 cup chopped onion
- 1 garlic clove, minced
- 2 teaspoons canola oil
- 2 cups cubed cooked meat loaf
- 1-1/2 cups cooked rice
- 1 cup salsa
- 1/4 cup minced fresh cilantro
- 1 teaspoon ground cumin
- 1/4 teaspoon salt

Pinch pepper
- 1/2 cup shredded Monterey Jack *or* cheddar cheese

Cut top off peppers and remove seeds. In a large saucepan, cook peppers in boiling water for 3 minutes. Drain and rinse in cold water; set aside.

In a large skillet, saute onion and garlic in oil until tender. Remove from the heat; add the meat loaf, rice, salsa, cilantro and cumin. Sprinkle inside of peppers with salt and pepper. Stuff with meat loaf mixture.

Place stuffed peppers in an ungreased 8-in. square baking dish. Bake, uncovered, at 350° for 20 minutes. Sprinkle with cheese. Bake 5 minutes longer or until cheese is melted. **Yield: 4 servings.**

CHEDDAR-SALSA BISCUIT STRIPS

A few ingredients are all you'll need to make these tender breadsticks that get their kick from salsa. I brought them to a wedding shower and got rave reviews. They're an excellent finger food for parties and equally good alongside soup or chili.
—Peggy Key, Grant, Alabama

1-2/3   cups self-rising flour
1   cup (4 ounces) shredded cheddar cheese
1/2   cup salsa
1/4   cup butter, melted
1/4   cup water
Additional melted butter, optional

In a large bowl, combine the flour and cheese. Stir in the salsa, butter and water just until combined. Turn the dough onto a floured surface; knead gently 6-8 times or until the dough is smooth.

Roll out into a 12-in. x 6-in. rectangle. Cut into 2-in. x 1-in. strips. Place 1 in. apart on a greased baking sheet.

Bake at 425° for 6-8 minutes or until golden brown. Brush with butter if desired. Remove from pan to wire racks. Serve warm. **Yield: about 3 dozen.**

Editor's Note: As a substitute for each cup of self-rising flour, place 1-1/2 teaspoons baking powder and 1/2 teaspoon salt in a measuring cup. Add all-purpose flour to measure 1 cup.

Easy Kitchen Tips

Be sure not to add too much flour to bread dough while kneading! To ensure perfect bread dough, simply follow this rule of thumb. As you knead the dough on a lightly floured surface, the dough will pick up a little more flour. Eventually it should feel smooth and satiny. If the dough is not sticking to your hands or kneading surface, do not add any more flour.

MEXICAN BREAD

MEXICAN BREAD

Chopped green chilies and flakes of red pepper provide flecks of color in every slice of this mouth-watering loaf. Slightly spicy with ground cumin, flavorful slices are great for sandwiches or as an accompaniment to homemade soups.
—Loni McCoy, Blaine, Minnesota

1   cup plus 2 tablespoons water (70° to 80°)
1/2   cup shredded Monterey Jack cheese
1   can (4 ounces) chopped green chilies
1   tablespoon butter, softened
2   tablespoons sugar
1   to 2 tablespoons crushed red pepper flakes
1   tablespoon nonfat dry milk powder
1   tablespoon ground cumin
1-1/2   teaspoons salt
3-1/4   cups bread flour
2-1/2   teaspoons active dry yeast

In a bread machine pan, place all ingredients in order suggested by manufacturer. Select basic bread setting. Choose crust color and loaf size if available.

Bake bread according to bread machine directions; (check the dough after 5 minutes of mixing; add 1 to 2 tablespoons of water or flour if needed). **Yield: 1 loaf (about 2 pounds).**

Editor's Note: We recommend you do not use a bread machine's time-delay feature for this recipe.

APPLE CHICKEN QUESADILLAS

APPLE CHICKEN QUESADILLAS

My sister came up with this easy recipe that can be served as a main course or an appetizer. People are surprised by the combination of chicken, apples, tomatoes and corn inside the crispy tortillas, but they love it.

—Stacia Slagle, Maysville, Missouri

2 medium tart apples, sliced
1 cup diced cooked chicken breast
1/2 cup shredded cheddar cheese
1/2 cup shredded part-skim mozzarella cheese
1/2 cup fresh *or* frozen corn, thawed
1/2 cup chopped fresh tomatoes
1/2 cup chopped onion
1/4 teaspoon salt
6 flour tortillas (8 inches), warmed
3/4 cup shredded lettuce
3/4 cup salsa
6 tablespoons sour cream

In a large bowl, combine the first eight ingredients. Place about 3/4 cup on half of each tortilla. Fold tortilla in half over filling and secure with toothpicks.

Place on a baking sheet coated with cooking spray. Bake at 400° for 8-10 minutes or until golden brown.

Carefully turn quesadillas over; bake 5-8 minutes longer or until golden brown. Discard toothpicks. Cut each quesadilla into three wedges. Serve with lettuce, salsa and sour cream. **Yield: 6 servings.**

SPANISH-STYLE BREAKFAST BAKE

Where I live in Texas, where there are a lot of Mexican and Spanish influences in the local cooking. This interesting combination of rice, chili sauce, eggs and green peppers really wakes up your taste buds in the morning.

—Dorothy Pritchett, Wills Point, Texas

4 cups cooked long grain rice
2 cups (8 ounces) shredded cheddar cheese, *divided*
12 bacon strips, cooked and crumbled, *divided*
1 can (15 ounces) tomato sauce
1/2 cup bottled chili sauce
12 eggs
12 thinly sliced green pepper rings

In a large bowl, combine the rice, 1-1/2 cups cheddar cheese, 1/2 cup bacon, tomato sauce and chili sauce. Pat firmly into a greased 13-in. x 9-in. baking dish.

Using the back of a spoon, make twelve 2-in. wells in the rice mixture. Cover and bake at 350° for 25 minutes.

Remove from the oven; break an egg into each well. Press a green pepper ring around each egg.

Cover and bake for another 30-35 minutes or until eggs reach desired doneness. Sprinkle with remaining cheese and bacon; cover and let stand 5-10 minutes or until cheese melts. **Yield: 12 servings.**

MEXICAN LASAGNA

If you're a fan of traditional pasta bakes, try this Southwestern version that feeds a large crowd. Tortilla strips replace the noodles and are layered with a zesty filling.

—Roma Rogers, Oshkosh, Nebraska

18 pounds ground beef
3 cups chopped onion
18 envelopes taco seasoning
6 cans (15 ounces *each*) tomato sauce
6 cans (14-1/2 ounces *each*) diced tomatoes, undrained
32 to 40 flour tortillas (10 inches), cut into 2-inch strips
4-1/2 pounds cheddar cheese, shredded, *divided*

In several Dutch ovens over medium heat, brown beef and onion; drain. Add the taco seasoning, tomato sauce and tomatoes; bring to a boil. Reduce heat; cover and simmer for 10 minutes.

Spoon about 2 cups each into six 13-in. x 9-in. baking pans. Top with a single layer of tortilla strips. Sprinkle with 1 cup cheese. Repeat layers two more times. Divide the remaining meat sauce among pans (each pan will have about 7 cups of sauce). Top with remaining tortillas.

Cover and bake at 350° for 40 minutes or until bubbly. Uncover; sprinkle with remaining cheese. Return to the oven for 5 to 10 minutes or until the cheese is melted. **Yield: 72 servings.**

BRUNCH ENCHILADAS

Taco seasoning and chopped green chilies lend a robust punch to these hearty egg-filled enchiladas. This baked brunch dish is a delicious change of pace from the usual fare.
—American Egg Board, Linda Braun, Park Ridge, Illinois

    8   hard-cooked eggs, chopped
    1   can (8-3/4 ounces) cream-style corn
  2/3   cup shredded cheddar cheese
    1   can (4 ounces) chopped green chilies
    2   teaspoons taco seasoning
  1/4   teaspoon salt
    8   corn tortillas, warmed
    1   bottle (8 ounces) mild taco sauce
Sour cream, optional

Combine the first six ingredients; spoon 1/2 cup down the center of each tortilla. Roll up tightly. Place, seam side down, in a greased 13-in. x 9-in. baking dish. Top with taco sauce.

Bake, uncovered, at 350° for 15 minutes or until heated through. Serve enchiladas with sour cream if desired. **Yield: 8 servings.**

SOUTHWESTERN STUFFED TURKEY BREAST

This turkey breast is a hit with family and friends around the holidays. The moist stuffing gives it a hint of Southwestern flair.
—Bernice Janowski, Stevens Point, Wisconsin

  1/3   cup sun-dried tomatoes (not packed in oil)
  2/3   cup boiling water
1-1/2   teaspoons dried oregano
    1   teaspoon salt
  3/4   teaspoon ground cumin
  1/2   teaspoon ground coriander
  1/4   teaspoon crushed red pepper flakes
    1   small onion, chopped
    1   small green pepper, diced
    1   garlic clove, minced
    1   tablespoon olive oil
    1   cup frozen corn, thawed
  1/2   cup dry bread crumbs
1-1/2   teaspoons grated lime peel
    1   boneless skinless turkey breast half (2 pounds)

Place tomatoes in a small bowl; cover with boiling water. Cover and let stand for 5 minutes. Drain, reserving 3 tablespoons liquid; set aside. Meanwhile, combine seasonings in a small bowl. Set aside.

In a large skillet, saute the tomatoes, onion, green pepper and garlic in oil until tender. Stir in corn and 2 teaspoons seasonings; remove from the heat. Stir in bread crumbs and reserved tomato liquid. Add lime peel to remaining seasonings; set side.

Cover turkey with plastic wrap. Flatten to 1/2-in. thickness; remove plastic. Sprinkle turkey with half of lime-seasoning mixture; spread vegetable mixture to within 1 in. of edges. Roll up jelly-roll style, starting with a short side; tie with kitchen string. Sprinkle with remaining lime-seasoning mixture. Place on a rack in a shallow roasting pan; cover loosely with foil.

Bake at 350° for 1 hour. Uncover; bake 15-30 minutes longer or until a meat thermometer reads 170°, basting occasionally with pan drippings. Let stand for 15 minutes before slicing. **Yield: 8 servings.**

SOUTHWESTERN STUFFED TURKEY BREAST

Desserts

TRES LECHES CAKE, P. 96

PIE PASTRY MEXICAN ICE CREAM

PIE PASTRY MEXICAN ICE CREAM

Refrigerated pie crust sprinkled with cinnamon sugar makes short work of this eye-catching, mouth-watering treat from our Test Kitchen. Keep a batch of these handy scoops in your freezer for impromptu entertaining all year long.

—Taste of Home Test Kitchen, Greendale, Wisconsin

    1   sheet refrigerated pie pastry
1-1/2   teaspoons sugar
    1   teaspoon ground cinnamon
    1   quart vanilla ice cream
  1/2   cup honey
Oil for frying

Unroll pastry onto an ungreased 15-in. x 10-in. baking pan. Combine sugar and cinnamon; sprinkle over pastry. Prick thoroughly with a fork. Bake at 400° for 10-12 minutes or until lightly browned. Cool pastry on a wire rack for 5 minutes.

Place pastry in a large resealable plastic bag; coarsely crush. Transfer to a shallow bowl. Using a 1/2-cup ice cream scoop, form eight scoops of ice cream. Roll in pastry crumbs. Cover and freeze for 2 hours or until firm.

In an electric skillet or deep-fat fryer, heat oil to 375°. Fry ice cream balls for 8-10 seconds or until golden. Drain on paper towels. Immediately place in chilled bowls; drizzle with honey and serve. **Yield: 8 servings.**

CARAMEL FLAN

Sometimes I like to top this traditional dessert with a dollop of whipped cream and toasted slivered almonds. The custard-like treat is a delicious finish to an authentic Mexican meal.

—Anelle Mack, Midland, Texas

  1/2   cup sugar
1-2/3   cups sweetened condensed milk
    1   cup milk
    3   eggs
    3   egg yolks
    1   teaspoon vanilla extract

In a large skillet over medium heat, cook the sugar until it is melted, about 12 minutes. Do not stir. When the sugar is melted, reduce heat to low and continue to cook, stirring occasionally, until the syrup is golden brown, about 2 minutes.

Quickly pour into an ungreased 2-qt. round souffle dish, tilting to coat the bottom; let stand for 10 minutes.

In a blender, combine the condensed milk, milk, eggs, yolks and vanilla. Cover and process for 15 seconds or until well blended. Slowly pour over syrup.

Place the souffle dish in a larger baking pan. Add 1 in. of boiling water to baking pan. Bake 350° for 55-60 minutes or until center is just set (mixture will jiggle). Remove souffle dish from larger pan. Place on a wire rack; cool for 1 hour. Cover and refrigerate overnight.

To unmold, run a knife around edge and invert flan onto a large rimmed serving platter. Cut into wedges or spoon onto dessert plates; spoon syrup over each serving. **Yield: 8-10 servings.**

CARAMEL FLAN

COFFEE CREAM TORTILLA CUPS

COFFEE CREAM TORTILLA CUPS

Here's a special dessert for two. Crispy tortilla bowls hold creamy coffee-flavored pudding topped with a mix of colorful fresh blueberries, raspberries and strawberries.
—Amber Zurbrugg, Alliance, Ohio

2	flour tortillas (8 inches), warmed
1	tablespoon butter, melted
1	tablespoon sugar
1/2	teaspoon ground cinnamon
1/2	cup half-and-half cream
2	teaspoons instant coffee granules
5	tablespoons instant French vanilla pudding mix
1	cup whipped topping
1-1/2	cups fresh blueberries, raspberries and sliced strawberries

Brush one side of tortillas with butter. Gently press each into a 10-oz. custard cup, buttered side up; pleat edges. Combine sugar and cinnamon; sprinkle over tortillas. Bake at 400° for 8-10 minutes or until tortillas are crisp and lightly browned. Cool on a wire rack.

In a small bowl, combine the cream and coffee granules until dissolved. Add pudding mix; whisk for 2 minutes. Let stand for 2 minutes or until soft-set. Fold in whipped topping. Cover and refrigerate for 1 hour. Spoon into tortilla cups. Top with berries. **Yield: 2 servings.**

MEXICAN WEDDING CAKES

As part of a Mexican tradition, I tucked these tender cookies into small gift boxes for the guests at my sister's wedding a few years ago. Most folks gobbled them up before they ever got home!
—Sarita Johnston, San Antonio, Texas

2	cups butter, softened
1	cup confectioners' sugar
4	cups all-purpose flour
1	teaspoon vanilla extract
1	cup finely chopped pecans

Additional confectioners' sugar

In a large bowl, cream butter and sugar until light and fluffy. Beat in vanilla. Gradually add flour until well combined. Stir in pecans.

Shape tablespoonfuls of dough into 2-in. crescents. Place crescents 2 in. apart on ungreased baking sheets. Bake at 350° for 12-15 minutes or until lightly browned. Roll the warm cookies in confectioners' sugar; cool on wire racks. **Yield: about 6 dozen.**

APRICOT BURRITOS

A sweet dessert burrito is stuffed with a delectable apricot and brown sugar filling that's spiced just right. It's sensational!
—Charl Sanchez, Roseville, California

1	cup chopped dried apricots
1	cup water
1/4	cup sugar
1/4	cup packed brown sugar
1/4	teaspoon ground cinnamon
1/4	teaspoon ground nutmeg
8	flour tortillas (6 inches)

Oil for frying
Cinnamon-sugar

In a large saucepan, combine the first six ingredients. Bring to a boil; reduce heat. Simmer, uncovered, for 10 minutes or until thickened. Place 1 tablespoon on each tortilla. Fold sides and ends over filling; roll up.

In an electric skillet, heat 1 in. of oil to 375°. Fry burritos, in batches, for 1 minute on each side or until golden brown. Drain on paper towels. Sprinkle the burritos with cinnamon-sugar. **Yield: 8 burritos.**

CINNAMON CHOCOLATE SUNDAES

Kids enjoy this tempting ice cream topping created by our home economists because it hardens on the ice cream. Store-bought sauces can't compare. The hint of cinnamon makes it a delicious ending to a Southwestern meal.

—Taste of Home Test Kitchen, Greendale, Wisconsin

- 1/2 cup butter
- 1/2 cup semisweet chocolate chips
- 1/3 cup packed brown sugar
- 1/4 cup corn syrup
- 1/4 cup half-and-half cream
- 1 teaspoon ground cinnamon
- 1 teaspoon vanilla extract
- Vanilla ice cream
- 1 cup chopped walnuts

In a small saucepan, combine the first five ingredients. Bring to a boil over medium-low heat, stirring constantly. Reduce heat; cook 5 minutes longer, stirring occasionally. Remove from the heat; stir in cinnamon and vanilla.

Transfer chocolate sauce to a heatproof measuring cup. Cool for 10 minutes, stirring occasionally. Pour sauce over ice cream; top with walnuts. Refrigerate leftover sauce. Rewarm sauce in a microwave before using. **Yield: 4 servings (about 1 cup sauce).**

FANTASTIC FLAN PIE

FANTASTIC FLAN PIE

The first time I made this creamy, slightly sweet pie, my friends and family raved about it. It's a deliciously different way to prepare the traditional Mexican dessert.

—Ireta Schoun, Montgomery, Michigan

- Pastry for single-crust pie (9 inches)
- 4 eggs
- 1 cup milk
- 1 can (14 ounces) sweetened condensed milk
- 1/2 cup sugar
- 1 teaspoon vanilla extract
- 1/2 teaspoon salt
- Fresh raspberries and blackberries

Line unpricked pastry with a double thickness of heavy-duty foil. Bake at 450° for 8 minutes. Remove foil; bake 5 minutes longer. Cool on a wire rack.

Meanwhile, in a blender, combine the eggs, milk, sweetened condensed milk, sugar, vanilla and salt; cover and process until smooth.

Pour filling into crust. Cover edges with foil. Bake at 400° for 15 minutes. Reduce heat to 350°; bake 20 minutes longer or until a knife inserted near the center comes out clean. Cool on a wire rack for 1 hour.

Cover and refrigerate until chilled. Garnish with fruit. Refrigerate leftovers. **Yield: 6-8 servings.**

CINNAMON CHOCOLATE SUNDAES

TRES LECHES CAKE

TRES LECHES CAKE

Tres Leches Cake, or Three Milk Cake, gets its name from the method of dipping pieces of delicate sponge cake in three different kinds of milk—evaporated, condensed and cream. Doing this gives the traditional Mexican dessert a distinct light and airy texture. We know you'll enjoy this version created by our Test Kitchen Staff.

—Taste of Home Test Kitchen, Greendale, Wisconsin

    4   eggs, *separated*
  2/3   cup sugar, *divided*
  2/3   cup cake flour
Dash salt
  3/4   cup heavy whipping cream
  3/4   cup evaporated milk
  3/4   cup sweetened condensed milk
    2   teaspoons vanilla extract
  1/4   teaspoon rum extract
TOPPING:
1-1/4   cups heavy whipping cream
    3   tablespoons sugar
Sliced fresh strawberries, optional

Let eggs stand at room temperature for 30 minutes. Line a 9-in. springform pan with waxed paper; grease and flour the paper. Set aside.

In a large bowl, beat egg yolks for 2 minutes. Add 1/3 cup sugar; beat for 3 minutes or until mixture is thick and lemon-colored. Fold in flour, a third at a time.

In another large bowl and with clean beaters, beat egg whites and salt on medium speed until soft peaks form. Gradually add remaining sugar, 1 tablespoon at a time,

beating on high until stiff peaks form. Stir a third of the whites into the yolk mixture. Fold in remaining whites.

Spread batter into prepared pan. Bake at 350° for 20-25 minutes or until top springs back when lightly touched. Cool for 10 minutes before removing from pan to a wire rack to cool completely.

In a small bowl, combine the cream, evaporated milk, condensed milk and extracts. Transfer cake to a serving plate. Poke holes in top of cake with a skewer. Gradually spoon milk mixture over top. Cover the cake and refrigerate for 2 hours.

For topping, in a small bowl, beat cream until it begins to thicken. Add sugar; beat until stiff peaks form. Spread topping over cake. Garnish cake with strawberries if desired. **Yield: 8-10 servings.**

CHOCOLATE CHIP QUESADILLA

I like to keep dessert sweet and simple...this yummy finale does the trick. It's a classic in my house because it's quick, different, deliciously chocolaty and requires just a handful of ingredients.

—Irene Rundell, Haskell, Oklahoma

    2   tablespoons honey
    2   flour tortillas (6 inches)
  1/2   teaspoon ground cinnamon
    2   tablespoons semisweet chocolate chips
    1   teaspoon canola oil

Drizzle honey over one tortilla; sprinkle with cinnamon and chocolate chips. Top with remaining tortilla.

In a small skillet, cook quesadilla in oil over medium heat for 1-2 minutes on each side or until lightly browned. Cut into four wedges. Serve immediately. **Yield: 2 servings.**

CHOCOLATE CHIP QUESADILLA

ICE CREAM TACOS

ICE CREAM TACOS

Talk about a fun presentation! The cute finale looks just like a taco—but it's stuffed with chocolate ice cream and topped with cherries and coconut instead of tomatoes and lettuce. You'll find they are as much fun to make as they are to eat.

—Karen Oney, Fort Worth, Texas

    2   flour tortillas (6 inches)
  1/8   teaspoon ground cinnamon
    2   tablespoons canola oil
    2   tablespoons chopped pecans
    2   tablespoons flaked coconut
    1   drop green food coloring
    1   cup chocolate ice cream
  1/4   cup whipped topping
    6   maraschino cherries, halved

Sprinkle one side of each tortilla with cinnamon. In a large skillet, heat tortillas, one at a time with cinnamon side up, in oil over medium heat. When tortilla starts to brown, fold into a taco shape; drain on paper towels.

In the same skillet, cook and stir the pecans for 2 minutes or until lightly toasted. Tint coconut with food coloring. Place two small scoops of ice cream in each tortilla shell; top with whipped topping, cherries, pecans and tinted coconut. **Yield: 2 servings.**

TORTILLA DESSERT CUPS

Diabetics and dessert lovers alike are "wowed" by these creamy treats. After finding out my mother had diabetes, I went on a search for good recipes like this. These bites taste so yummy, no one will ever guess they're low in anything!

—Susan Miller, Wakeman, Ohio

    3   tablespoons sugar
    2   teaspoons ground cinnamon
   10   flour tortillas (6 inches)
    1   package (8 ounces) reduced-fat cream cheese
    1   cup cold fat-free milk
    1   package (1 ounce) sugar-free instant white chocolate *or* vanilla pudding mix
    2   cups reduced-fat whipped topping
  1/4   cup milk chocolate chips, melted

In a small bowl, combine sugar and cinnamon. Coat one side of each tortilla with cooking spray; sprinkle with cinnamon-sugar. Turn tortillas over; repeat on the other side. Cut each tortilla into four wedges.

For each dessert cup, place round edge of one tortilla wedge in the bottom of a muffin cup, shaping sides to fit cup. Place a second tortilla wedge in muffin cup, allowing bottom and sides to overlap. Bake at 350° for 10 minutes or until crisp and lightly browned. Cool completely in pan.

Meanwhile, for filling, in a small bowl, beat cream cheese until smooth. In another bowl, whisk milk and pudding mix for 2 minutes. Let stand for 2 minutes or until soft-set. Beat in cream cheese on low until smooth. Fold in whipped topping. Cover and refrigerate for 1 hour.

Carefully remove cups from pan. Pipe or spoon about 3 tablespoons filling into each cup. Drizzle or pipe with melted chocolate. Refrigerate for 5 minutes or until chocolate is set. Store dessert cups in the refrigerator. **Yield: 20 servings.**

TORTILLA DESSERT CUPS

FRUITY CHOCOLATE TORTILLA BOWLS

FRUITY CHOCOLATE TORTILLA BOWLS

These south-of-the-border treats are a meal-ending favorite with my family. You'll love the presentation of strawberries, apricots, peaches and plums in chocolate-drizzled tortilla cups.

—Marion Karlin, Waterloo, Iowa

   1   to 2 tablespoons butter, softened
   8   flour tortillas (6 inches), warmed
3/4   cup semisweet chocolate chips
   1   teaspoon shortening
FILLING:
   1   pound fresh apricots, halved
   2   tablespoons honey
1-1/2   cups halved fresh strawberries
   3   small plums, sliced
   2   medium peaches, sliced
1/2   cup heavy whipping cream
   2   tablespoons confectioners' sugar

Spread butter over one side of each tortilla. Press tortillas, butter side down, into ungreased 8-oz. custard cups. Place on a 15-in. x 10-in. baking pan. Bake at 400° for 10-12 minutes or until golden brown. Remove tortilla from custard cups; cool on wire racks.

In a microwave-safe bowl, melt chocolate chips and shortening; stir until smooth. Drizzle over insides of tortilla cups; refrigerate for 3-4 minutes or until set.

For filling, in a food processor, combine apricots and honey; cover and process until smooth. In a large bowl, combine the strawberries, plums and peaches; add apricot mixture and gently toss to coat. Spoon 1/2 cup into each tortilla cup.

In a small bowl, beat cream until it begins to thicken. Add confectioners' sugar; beat until stiff peaks form. Dollop onto fruit. **Yield: 8 servings.**

CINNAMON CHIPS 'N' DIP

A friend shared this addicting treat. We lightened it up and created this equally delicious version. It's a great beginning or a special ending to a Southwestern meal.

—Krista Frank, Rhododendron, Oregon

   4   flour tortillas (8 inches)
Refrigerated butter-flavored spray
   1   tablespoon sugar
   1   teaspoon ground cinnamon
DIP:
   4   ounces reduced-fat cream cheese
   1   carton (6 ounces) vanilla yogurt
4-1/2   teaspoons sugar
1/2   teaspoon ground cinnamon

For chips, spritz tortillas with butter-flavored spray; cut each into eight wedges. Place on ungreased baking sheets. Combine sugar and cinnamon; sprinkle over tortillas. Bake at 350° for 7-9 minutes or just until crisp.

Meanwhile, for dip, in a small bowl, beat the cream cheese, yogurt, sugar and cinnamon until smooth. Serve with cinnamon chips. **Yield: 8 servings.**

CINNAMON CHIPS 'N' DIP

BLUEBERRY/KIWI FLAN

This is a recipe that is fun to make, pretty to serve and tastes good, too. It is also versatile—feel free to mix and match whatever fruits are your family's favorites.

—Pollie Malone, Ames, Iowa

CRUST:
- 1/2   cup sugar
- 1/2   cup confectioners' sugar
- 1/2   cup butter
- 1/2   cup canola oil
- 1   egg
- 2   cups plus 2 tablespoons flour
- 1/2   teaspoon cream of tartar
- 1/2   teaspoon baking soda
- 1/2   teaspoon vanilla extract

CREAM CHEESE FILLING:
- 1   package (8 ounces) cream cheese
- 1/3   cup sugar
- 1   teaspoon vanilla extract

FRUIT LAYER:
- 3   cups fresh blueberries
- 2   medium kiwifruit, peeled and thinly sliced

CITRUS GLAZE:
- 1/2   cup water
- 1/2   cup orange juice
- 2   tablespoons lemon juice
- 1/4   cup sugar
- 1   tablespoon cornstarch

In a large bowl, combine the crust ingredients together until blended. Divide dough in half; press onto the bottom and up the sides of greased two 12-in. pizza pans or tart pans with removable bottoms.

Bake at 350° for 10-12 minutes or until the crust is golden brown. Cool. Carefully remove one crust to a round platter. Freeze the other crust for later use. Crust may be frozen for up to 3 months.

In a large bowl, cream together cheese filling ingredients; spread on crust. Spread blueberries and kiwi on top of cheese layer in decorative pattern. Refrigerate.

For glaze, in a small saucepan, combining all the glaze ingredients; bring to a boil. Cook and stir for 1 minute or until thickened; cool. Spread over fruit layer; refrigerate until serving time. **Yield: 16-20 servings.**

Editor's Note: You may substitute refrigerated sugar cookie dough for the crust.

MEXICAN ICE CREAM SUNDAES

MEXICAN ICE CREAM SUNDAES

This fiesta dinner finale makes an impressive presentation. The tortillas take on a subtle flavor when sprinkled with cinnamon-sugar.

—Milbert Fichter, Pittsburgh, Pennsylvania

- 1/2   cup canola oil
- 6   flour tortillas (6 inches), cut into 6 wedges *each*
- 2   tablespoons sugar
- 1/2   teaspoon ground cinnamon
- 1/4   cup crushed cornflakes
- 6   large scoops vanilla ice cream

Chocolate syrup, optional

Whipped cream in a can
- 6   maraschino cherries with stems

In a large skillet, heat oil over medium heat. Fry the tortilla wedges, a few at a time, for 1-2 minutes on each side or until crisp. Drain tortilla wedges on paper towels. Combine the sugar and cinnamon; set aside 1 tablespoon. Sprinkle both sides of tortillas, with the remaining cinnamon-sugar mixture.

In a shallow bowl, combine the cornflake crumbs and reserved cinnamon-sugar. Roll ice cream in crumb mixture to coat. Freeze until serving.

Drizzle serving plates with chocolate syrup if desired. Place six tortilla wedges on each plate; top each with a scoop of ice cream. Pipe whipped cream around base and on top of ice cream. Garnish each ice cream scoop with a cherry. **Yield: 6 servings.**

CARAMEL APPLE BURRITOS

CARAMEL APPLE BURRITOS

If you love the taste of caramel apples, you will adore this sweet, gooey dessert that packs that popular flavor into soft flour tortillas. Three ingredients make it a breeze to prepare.
—Cindy Reams, Philipsburg, Pennsylvania

    3   large tart apples, peeled and sliced
   10   caramels
    5   flour tortillas (8 inches), warmed

Place apple slices in a saucepan; cover and cook over medium heat for 3-4 minutes or until apple slices are tender. Reduce heat.

Add caramels; cook and stir until caramels are melted. Spoon apple mixture off center on each tortilla; fold sides and ends over filling and roll up. **Yield: 5 servings.**

NOT-FRIED ICE CREAM CAKE

Our home economists created this ice cream cake to mimic the fabulous flavor of a popular dessert served in many Mexican restaurants. It's a no-fuss treat that feeds a crowd. Plus, it's conveniently made ahead.
—Taste of Home Test Kitchen, Greendale, Wisconsin

      1   cup cornflake crumbs
    1/3   cup sugar
    1/3   cup butter, melted
    3/4   teaspoon ground cinnamon
    1/2   gallon butter pecan ice cream, softened
      4   tablespoons honey, *divided*

In a small bowl, combine the cornflake crumbs, sugar, butter and cinnamon; set aside 1/2 cup. Press remaining crumb mixture into a greased 9-in. springform pan.

Spoon half of the ice cream over crust. Sprinkle with reserved crumb mixture; drizzle with 2 tablespoons honey. Cover and freeze for 2 hours.

Top with remaining ice cream. Cover and freeze for 8 hours or overnight.

Remove from the freezer 5 minutes before serving. Remove sides of pan; drizzle with remaining honey. **Yield: 12-16 servings.**

MEXICAN HOT COCOA

Warm up to a mug of this rich, chocolaty cocoa. The hint of cinnamon makes it delightfully different.
—Stella Gilbertson, Northfield, Minnesota

     12   cups water
      3   to 4 cinnamon sticks (3 inches)
      2   cans (16 ounces *each*) chocolate syrup
      3   cans (12 ounces *each*) evaporated milk
      1   can (14 ounces) sweetened condensed milk
  1-1/2   teaspoons vanilla extract
Whipped cream, ground cinnamon and cinnamon
    sticks, optional

In a large kettle, combine water and cinnamon sticks. Bring mixture to a boil; reduce heat, cover and simmer for 10-15 minutes or until liquid turns light brown. Remove cinnamon sticks and discard.

In another bowl, combine the chocolate syrup, milks and vanilla; slowly stir into cinnamon water. Return mixture to a simmer just to heat through. Top servings with whipped cream, cinnamon and cinnamon sticks if desired. **Yield: about 5 quarts.**

MEXICAN HOT COCOA

CHILI PEPPER COOKIES

In a small bowl, beat the butter, confectioners' sugar, vanilla and enough milk until frosting reaches desired consistency. Tint 1/3 cup green; set aside. Tint remaining frosting red. Frost "peppers" red and "stems" green; sprinkle with matching sugar. **Yield: about 4 dozen.**

PEACH CHIMMIES

I developed these treats for our town's peach festival. They are timely, easy and wonderfully refreshing. As a variation, I sometimes use peach pie filling instead of diced peaches.
—Karolyn Czyz, Lewiston, New York

- 2   flour tortillas (6 inches), warmed
- 2   tablespoons cream cheese, softened
- 1   snack-size cup (4 ounces) diced peaches, drained
- 1/8 teaspoon ground cinnamon

Oil for frying

Whipped cream, caramel ice cream topping, confectioners' sugar *or* additional peaches, optional

Spread tortillas with cream cheese. Combine peaches and cinnamon; spoon down the center of each tortilla. Fold sides and ends over filling and roll up.

In an electric skillet or deep-fat fryer, heat 1 in. of oil to 375°. Fry chimmies for 1 minute on each side or until golden brown. Drain on paper towels. Serve warm.

Garnish with whipped cream, drizzle with caramel topping, dust with confectioners' sugar or serve with additional peaches if desired. **Yield: 2 servings.**

CHILI PEPPER COOKIES

These soft, tender cut-out sugar cookies are shaped and decorated to look like chili peppers. The fun-to-make nibbles are a great way to get your kids involved in the kitchen.
—Terri Newton, Marshall, Texas

- 3/4   cup butter-flavored shortening
- 1   cup packed brown sugar
- 1/4   cup sugar
- 1   egg
- 2   tablespoons milk
- 1   tablespoon vanilla extract
- 2-1/4 cups all-purpose flour
- 3/4   teaspoon baking soda
- 1/8   teaspoon salt

BUTTERCREAM FROSTING:
- 1/2   cup butter, softened
- 4-1/2 cups confectioners' sugar
- 2   teaspoons vanilla extract
- 3   to 5 tablespoons milk

Green and red gel food coloring
Green and red colored sugar

In a small bowl, cream shortening and sugars until light and fluffy. Beat in the egg, milk and vanilla. Combine the flour, baking soda and salt; gradually add to creamed mixture and mix well. Cover and refrigerate for 2 hours or until easy to handle.

On a lightly floured surface, roll and pat out dough to 1/4-in. thickness. Cut with a floured 3-1/2-in. chili pepper shaped cookie cutter.

Place 1 in. apart on ungreased baking sheets. Bake at 325° for 6-8 minutes or until edges are lightly browned. Remove to wire racks to cool.

PEACH CHIMMIES

CINNAMON CHOCOLATE NACHOS

CINNAMON CHOCOLATE NACHOS

Here is a "sweet" way to serve nachos. The buttery crisps topped with an irresistible chocolate sauce and crunchy pecans disappear fast, so be sure to have plenty on hand.
—Kathy Kittell, Lenexa, Kansas

  6   flour tortillas (8 inches)
  7   tablespoons butter, melted, *divided*
  6   tablespoons sugar, *divided*
1/2 teaspoon ground cinnamon
1/2 cup heavy whipping cream
1/3 cup packed brown sugar
  1   square (1 ounce) unsweetened chocolate, chopped
1/2 teaspoon vanilla extract
1/2 cup chopped pecans

Brush both sides of tortillas with 4 tablespoons butter. Combine 2 tablespoons sugar and cinnamon; sprinkle over one side of each tortilla. Stack tortillas, sugared side up; cut into 12 wedges. Arrange in a single layer on baking sheets. Bake at 350° for 12-14 minutes or until crisp.

Meanwhile, in a heavy saucepan, combine the cream, brown sugar and remaining butter and sugar. Bring to a boil over medium heat, stirring constantly. Cook and stir for 5 minutes or until slightly thickened. Remove from the heat; stir in chocolate and vanilla. Cool slightly.

Arrange half of the tortilla wedges on a large serving platter. Drizzle tortilla wedges with half of the chocolate sauce; sprinkle with half of the pecans. Repeat layers.
Yield: 12 servings.

THREE MILK CAKE

With a large Hispanic population here, I have found the best recipes for Mexican food. This traditional dessert is a cross between cake and pudding.
—Janice Montiverdi, Sugar Land, Texas

  6   eggs, *separated*
1-1/2 cups sugar
  2   cups all-purpose flour
  2   teaspoons baking powder
1/2 teaspoon baking soda
1/2 teaspoon salt
1-1/2 cups water
  1   teaspoon almond extract
TOPPING:
  1   can (14 ounces) sweetened condensed milk
  2   cups heavy whipping cream
1/2 cup light corn syrup
  7   tablespoons evaporated milk
  2   teaspoons vanilla extract
ICING:
1/2 cup heavy whipping cream
1/2 cup sugar
  1   teaspoon vanilla extract
  1   cup (8 ounces) sour cream
  2   tablespoons confectioners' sugar
  1   teaspoon almond extract

In a large bowl, beat egg whites until soft peaks form. Gradually beat in sugar until stiff peaks form. Add yolks, one at a time, beating until combined. Combine the flour, baking powder, baking soda and salt; add to egg mixture alternately with water. Stir in extract.

Pour into a greased 13-in. x 9-in. baking dish. Bake at 350° for 35-45 minutes or until a toothpick inserted near the center comes out clean. Cool on a wire rack. Poke holes in cake with a fork. Chill overnight.

In a large saucepan, combine the condensed milk, cream, corn syrup and evaporated milk. Bring to a boil over medium heat, stirring constantly; cook and stir for 2 minutes or until thickened.

Remove from the heat; stir in vanilla. Slowly pour milk mixture over chilled cake, letting milk absorb into cake. Cover cake and refrigerate.

In a small bowl, beat cream until soft peaks form. Gradually beat in sugar until stiff peaks form. Stir in vanilla. In a large bowl, combine the sour cream, confectioners' sugar and extract. Fold in whipped cream. Spread frosting over sides and top of cake. Refrigerate until serving. **Yield: 12-15 servings.**

MEXICAN FRIED ICE CREAM

MEXICAN FRIED ICE CREAM

Fried ice cream is one of my favorite desserts to order when eating at a Mexican restaurant. When my sister and I found this recipe for preparing it at home, we knew it would be an impressive way to end a meal. It tastes like a restaurant specialty.
—Mandy Wright, Springville, Utah

1/2 gallon French vanilla ice cream, softened
3 cups crushed cornflakes
4 teaspoons ground cinnamon
Oil for frying
Honey and whipped topping, optional

Place nine 3-in. scoops of ice cream on a baking sheet. Freeze for 1 hour or until firm.

In a shallow bowl, combine cornflake crumbs and cinnamon. Roll ice cream balls in crumb mixture. Place on baking sheet and freeze overnight or wrap each scoop in plastic wrap and place in a freezer bag. May be frozen for up to 2 months.

When ready to use, in an electric skillet or deep-fat fryer, heat oil to 375°. Unwrap ice cream; fry one scoop at a time for 8-10 seconds. Place in chilled bowls. Drizzle with honey and garnish with whipped topping if desired. **Yield: 9 servings.**

APPLE CHEESE WRAPS

These tortilla-wrapped apple and cheese treats are a light alternative to apple pie and a unique brunch item. You can also substitute Granny Smith apples for the Golden Delicious variety. If you really want to splurge, top the warm wraps with a scoop of vanilla frozen yogurt or low-fat ice cream.
—Grace Malone, Lafayette, Colorado

1 tablespoon butter
1/4 cup packed brown sugar
3 cups thinly sliced peeled Golden Delicious apples (about 2 medium)
1/4 cup golden raisins
1/2 teaspoon ground cinnamon
1/8 teaspoon ground nutmeg
1/2 teaspoon vanilla extract
5 flour tortillas (8 inches), warmed
1/3 cup shredded reduced-fat cheddar cheese
TOPPING:
1/2 teaspoon sugar
Dash ground cinnamon
10 tablespoons reduced-fat whipped topping

In a small saucepan, melt the butter over medium-low heat; stir in the brown sugar until dissolved. Add the apple slices, raisins, cinnamon and nutmeg. Cook and stir apple mixture over medium heat until the apples are tender. Remove from the heat; stir in the vanilla extract. Cool slightly.

Place each tortilla on a 12-in. square piece of foil. Top each tortilla with about 1/4 cup apple mixture; sprinkle with shredded cheddar cheese. Fold in the sides of the tortilla and roll up. Wrap in foil.

Bake wraps at 350° for 10-12 minutes or until heated through. Combine the sugar and cinnamon; sprinkle cinnamon-sugar mixture over the wraps. Serve warm with whipped topping. **Yield: 5 servings.**

Easy Kitchen Tips

When scooping ice cream from the carton, do so quickly and return the unused portion to the freezer as soon as possible. Thawing and refreezing causes ice crystals to form on the surface of the ice cream. It is also a good idea to store the ice cream in the coldest part of the freezer away from the door.

CINNAMON CHOCOLATE CHIP ICE CREAM

CINNAMON CHOCOLATE CHIP ICE CREAM

I was first served this creamy, soft-set ice cream at a friend's house. A hint of cinnamon is the secret ingredient.

—Gloria Heidner, Elk River, Minnesota

   2   cups heavy whipping cream
   2   cups half-and-half cream
   1   cup sugar
 1/2   cup chocolate syrup
1-1/2   teaspoons vanilla extract
 1/4   teaspoon ground cinnamon
Pinch salt
 1/2   cup miniature semisweet chocolate chips
Additional miniature semisweet chocolate chips

In a large bowl, combine the first seven ingredients; stir until the sugar is dissolved. Fill cylinder of ice cream freezer two-thirds full; freeze according to the manufacturer's directions. Stir in chocolate chips.

Refrigerate remaining mixture until ready to freeze. Allow to ripen in ice cream freezer or firm up in your refrigerator freezer 2-4 hours before serving. Sprinkle with additional chips. **Yield: about 2 quarts.**

ANISE BUTTER COOKIES

Here in New Mexico, these cookies are known as "bizcochitos," which means "small biscuit." There are many variations of the recipe, which has been passed down through the generations. The cookies are enjoyed during the holidays and at wedding receptions and other special celebrations.

—Mari Lynn Van Ginkle, Sandia Park, New Mexico

   2   cups butter, softened
1-3/4   cups sugar, *divided*
   2   eggs
 1/4   cup orange juice concentrate
   4   teaspoons aniseed, crushed
   6   cups all-purpose flour
   3   teaspoons baking powder
 1/2   teaspoon salt
   1   teaspoon ground cinnamon

In a large bowl, cream the butter and 1-1/2 cups sugar until light and fluffy. Add eggs, one at a time, beating well after each addition. Beat in orange juice concentrate and aniseed.

Combine the flour, baking powder and salt; gradually add to creamed mixture and mix well.

On a lightly floured surface, roll out dough to 1/4-in. thickness. Cut with a floured 2-1/2-in. round cookie cutter. Place 1 in. apart on ungreased baking sheets.

Combine the cinnamon and remaining sugar; sprinkle over cookies. Bake at 350° for 12-15 minutes or until golden brown. Remove to wire racks. **Yield: 5 dozen.**

MEXICAN CHOCOLATE CRINKLES

I love to bake. In fact, my first try at baking "from scratch" is still vivid in my memory. This recipe brings back memories, too. When our two girls were young, they often took these cookies to their Scout outings.

—Pat Gregory, Tulsa, Oklahoma

 3/4   cup shortening
   1   cup sugar
   1   egg
 1/4   cup light corn syrup
   1   square (1 ounce) unsweetened chocolate, melted
1-3/4   cups all-purpose flour
   2   teaspoons baking soda
 1/4   teaspoon salt
   1   teaspoon ground cinnamon
Additional sugar

In a large bowl, cream shortening and sugar until light and fluffy. Add the egg, corn syrup and melted chocolate. Combine flour, baking soda, salt and cinnamon; gradually add to creamed mixture and mix well.

Roll into walnut-sized balls and roll in sugar; place 3 in. apart on ungreased baking sheets. Bake at 350° for 10-12 minutes (cookies should by soft). Cool 2-3 minutes before removing to wire racks. **Yield: 2-1/2 dozen.**

QUICKER CARAMEL FLAN

QUICKER CARAMEL FLAN

If you enjoy flan, but don't want to spend a lot of time in the kitchen, turn to this quick and simple version of the traditional Mexican specialty created by our home economists.

—Taste of Home Test Kitchen, Greendale, Wisconsin

5	eggs
1/2	cup sugar
1	teaspoon vanilla extract
1/8	teaspoon salt
2-1/2	cups milk
2	tablespoons caramel ice cream topping

In a small bowl, whisk the eggs, sugar, vanilla and salt. Gradually stir in milk. Spoon 1 teaspoon caramel topping into each of six ungreased 6-oz. custard cups.

Place cups in a 13-in. x 9-in. baking dish. Pour egg mixture into each cup (cups will be full). Fill baking dish with 1 in. of hot water.

Bake, uncovered, at 350° for 30-35 minutes or until the centers are almost set (mixture will jiggle). Remove custard cups from the water to a wire rack; let cool for 30 minutes.

Refrigerate for 3 hours or until flan is thoroughly chilled. Invert custard cups and unmold onto rimmed dessert dishes. **Yield: 6 servings.**

CINNAMON MOCHA COFFEE

One snowy day, my neighbor called and invited me over to try a new beverage she'd made. It was delicious! This spiced coffee is a comforting sipper any time of year.

—Bernice Morris, Marshfield, Missouri

1/2	cup ground dark roast coffee
1	tablespoon ground cinnamon
1/4	teaspoon ground nutmeg
5	cups water
1	cup milk
1/3	cup chocolate syrup
1/4	cup packed brown sugar
1	teaspoon vanilla extract

Whipped cream, optional

In a small bowl, combine coffee grounds, cinnamon and nutmeg; pour into coffee filter of a drip coffeemaker. Add water; brew coffee according to manufacturer's directions.

In a large saucepan, combine the milk, chocolate syrup and brown sugar. Cook over low heat until sugar is dissolved, stirring occasionally. Stir in the vanilla and brewed coffee.

Ladle into mugs; garnish with whipped cream if desired. **Yield: 6 servings.**

CINNAMON MOCHA COFFEE

FROSTY CARAMEL TREAT

occasionally. Add butter. Gradually add milk, stirring constantly. Cook and stir for 8 minutes or until sauce is thick and golden; keep warm.

Heat oil in an electric skillet or deep-fat fryer to 375°. Fry ice cream balls until golden, about 30 seconds. Drain on paper towels. Serve immediately with caramel sauce. **Yield: 8 servings.**

BROWN SUGAR PECAN CANDIES

These sweet candies are similar to those served at Mexican restaurants in our area. The recipe comes from a cookbook put together by the staff of the school where I teach.

—Barbara Windham, Houston, Texas

1-1/2	cups sugar
1/2	cup packed brown sugar
1/2	cup evaporated milk
3	tablespoons light corn syrup
4	large marshmallows, cut into quarters
2	tablespoons butter
2	cups coarsely chopped pecans
1/2	teaspoon vanilla extract

In a large heavy saucepan, combine the sugars, milk and corn syrup. Cook over medium-low heat, stirring occasionally, until a candy thermometer reads 238° (soft-ball stage).

Remove from the heat; stir in marshmallows and butter until smooth. Add pecans and vanilla; stir only until mixture begins to thicken. Quickly drop by tablespoonfuls onto waxed paper. Cool until set. Store in an airtight container at room temperature. **Yield: 5 dozen.**

Editor's Note: We recommend that you test your candy thermometer before each use by bringing water to a boil; the thermometer should read 212°. Adjust your recipe temperature up or down based on your test.

RICH CHOCOLATE WRAPS

Never thought of using a tortilla to wrap something sweet? This novel indulgence created by our Test Kitchen Staff will make a believer out of everyone from the first bite. Its creamy filling has a wonderfully rich taste.

—Taste of Home Test Kitchen, Greendale, Wisconsin

FROSTY CARAMEL TREAT

For birthday parties or outdoor barbecues, this cool and creamy treat is always a favorite. I sometimes substitute strawberry or Neopolitan for the vanilla ice cream. Go ahead and substitute the flavor that your family likes best.

—Darlene Brenden, Salem, Oregon

1	quart vanilla ice cream
1/4	cup heavy whipping cream
2	teaspoons vanilla extract
2	cups flaked coconut, finely chopped
2	cups finely crushed cornflakes
1/2	teaspoon ground cinnamon

CARAMEL SAUCE:

1	cup sugar
1/2	cup butter, cubed
1/2	cup evaporated milk

Oil for frying

Using a 1/2-cup ice cream scoop, place eight scoops of ice cream on a baking sheet. Cover and freeze ice cream for 2 hours or until firm. In a bowl, combine whipping cream and vanilla extract. In another bowl, combine flaked coconut, cornflakes and cinnamon.

Remove scoops of ice cream from freezer; wearing plastic gloves, shape the ice cream into balls. Dip balls into cream mixture, then roll in coconut mixture, making sure to coat entire surface. Place coated balls on a baking sheet. Cover and freeze at least 3 hours or until firm.

For caramel sauce, heat sugar in a heavy saucepan over medium heat until partially melted and golden, stirring

1/2 cup miniature semisweet chocolate chips
2 teaspoons butter
1 cup (8 ounces) sour cream
1 tablespoon confectioners' sugar
1/4 to 1/2 teaspoon ground cinnamon
6 flour tortillas (6 inches)
Baking cocoa

In a microwave, melt the chocolate chips and butter; stir until smooth. Cool slightly. In a small bowl, beat the sour cream, sugar and cinnamon until blended; stir in the melted chocolate.

Spread about 3 tablespoons chocolate mixture over each tortilla. Roll up tightly and wrap in plastic wrap. Refrigerate for 1 hour. Sprinkle tortillas with baking cocoa before serving. **Yield: 6 servings.**

PENUCHE

My mom used to make this brown sugar fudge every year during the holidays, both for our family and to give as gifts. It has such wonderful old-fashioned flavor. We still savor this timeless tradition today.

—Rosemarie Anderson, Great Valley, New York

2 cups packed brown sugar
1 cup sugar
1 cup half-and-half cream
2 tablespoons light corn syrup
1 teaspoon lemon juice
Pinch salt
2 tablespoons butter
1 teaspoon vanilla extract
1/2 cup chopped pecans

In a large heavy saucepan, combine the sugars, cream, corn syrup, lemon juice and salt. Bring to a boil over medium heat, stirring occasionally.

Cook, without stirring, until a candy thermometer reads 238° (soft-ball stage). Hold at soft-ball stage for 5-6 minutes. Remove mixture from the heat. Add butter; do not stir. Cool to 110°.

Stir in vanilla; beat vigorously by hand until the mixture is very thick and slightly lighter in color, about 20 minutes. Quickly stir in the pecans, then pour into a greased 8-in. square pan. Cool. Cut fudge into 1-in. squares. **Yield: 1-3/4 pounds.**

SOPAIPILLAS

Light, crispy pastry puffs, sopaipillas are a sweet way to round out a spicy meal. They make a nice winter dessert served warm and topped with honey or sugar.

—Mary Anne McWhirter, Pearland, Texas

1 cup all-purpose flour
1-1/2 teaspoons baking powder
1/4 teaspoon salt
1 tablespoon shortening
1/3 cup warm water
Oil for frying
Honey, optional
Confectioners' sugar, optional

In a large bowl, combine flour, baking powder and salt. Cut in shortening until mixture resembles fine crumbs. Gradually add water, tossing with a fork until a loose ball forms (dough will be crumbly).

On a lightly floured surface, knead dough for 3 minutes or until smooth. Cover and let rest for 10 minutes. Roll out dough into a 12-in. x 10-in. rectangle. Cut dough into 12 squares.

In a deep-fat fryer, heat 2 in. of oil to 375°. Fry sopaipillas for 1 to 2 minutes per side. Drain on paper towels; keep warm. Serve with honey or dust with confectioners' sugar if desired. **Yield: 6-8 servings.**

SOPAIPILLAS

General Recipe Index

This index lists every recipe by food category and/or major ingredient,
so you can easily locate recipes to suit your needs.

Alphabetical Index

This index lists every recipe in alphabetical order so you can easily
find your favorite recipes.

G

Green Chili 'n' Rice Casserole, 84
Green Chili Flautas, 57
Green Chili Pork Stew, 27
Green Chili Rice, 49
Green Chili Stew, 23
Green Chili Tomato Soup, 37
Grilled Corn Salsa, 21
Grilled Fajitas, 64
Grilled Pork and Poblano Peppers, 61
Grilled Shrimp Fajitas, 70

H

Hobo Stew, 37
Hominy Taco Chili, 34
Hot Green Rice, 50
Hot Mexican Dip, 9
Hot Tamale Pie, 88

I

Ice Cream Tacos, 97

J

Jalapeno Bread, 88
Jalapeno Chicken Enchiladas, 60
Jalapeno Poppers, 17

L

Loaded Tortillas, 21

M

Meaty Corn Bread Squares, 78
Mexican Bread, 87
Mexican Chicken Corn Chowder, 31
Mexican Chocolate Crinkles, 104
Mexican Fried Ice Cream, 103
Mexican Hot Cocoa, 100
Mexican Ice Cream Sundaes, 99
Mexican Lasagna, 90
Mexican Meat Loaf, 84
Mexican Omelet, 86
Mexican Shrimp Bisque, 35
Mexican-Style Pork Chops, 70
Mexican Sunset Bread, 89
Mexican Wedding Cakes, 94
Microwave Texas Nachos, 7
Mock Strawberry Margaritas, 20
Mole Poblano, 10
Mole Poblano de Guajolote, 64
Mom's Paella, 77

N

Nacho Pie, 84
Not-Fried Ice Cream Cake, 100

P

Peach Chimmies, 101

Peachy Avocado Salsa, 12
Penuche, 107
Pepper Jack Batter Bread, 83
Pepper Jack Potatoes, 43
Pepper Steak Quesadillas, 63
Peppered Cilantro Rice, 44
Peppy Peach Salsa, 16
Pie Pastry Fried Ice Cream, 93
Pineapple Chicken Fajitas, 57
Pineapple Mango Salsa, 14
Pork 'n' Pepper Tacos, 56
Pork Carnitas, 73
Pork Fajita Kabobs, 66
Posole, 24

Q

Quicker Caramel Flan, 105

R

Ranch Beans, 44
Red Beans 'n' Brown Rice, 45
Refreshing Lemon-Lime Drink, 5
Rich Chocolate Wraps, 106
Roasted Veggie Chili, 36

S

Salmon Quesadillas, 59
Salsa Chicken Soup, 31
Salsa Corn Cakes, 43
Salsa Pasta 'n' Beans, 42
Salsa Rice with Zucchini, 52
Salsa Sausage Quiche, 85
Salsa Verde, 8
Sangria, 10
Santa Fe Cheesecake, 18
Santa Fe Chicken, 78
Santa Fe Stew, 25
Sausage Fajitas, 59
Seafood Nachos, 19
Simple Taco Soup, 24
Soft Chicken Tacos, 71
Sopa de Tortilla, 28
Sopaipillas, 107
Sopes, 5
Southwest Barley Stew, 29
Southwest Pork and Bean Salad, 50
Southwest Scallop Salad, 48
Southwest Skillet Corn, 50
Southwest Stuffed Chicken, 75
Southwest Stuffed Peppers, 86
Southwest Vegetarian Bake, 81
Southwestern Barley Salad, 42
Southwestern Chicken Salad, 41
Southwestern Chicken Soup, 26
Southwestern Deep-Dish Pizza, 76
Southwestern Egg Rolls, 14
Southwestern Hash, 80

Southwestern Meat and Potato Stew, 32
Southwestern Onion Rings, 6
Southwestern Salad, 45
Southwestern Seafood Egg Rolls, 13
Southwestern Stuffed Turkey Breast, 91
Southwestern Veggie Salad, 53
Spanish-Style Breakfast Bake, 90
Spicy Chicken Rice Soup, 36
Spicy Creamed Corn, 45
Spicy Spanish Rice, 51
Spicy Steak Stew, 30
Spinach Chicken Enchiladas, 65
Steak Tortillas, 65
Stuffed Banana Peppers, 8
Stuffed Jalapenos, 11
Stuffed Roast Pepper Soup, 33
Sweet 'n' Savory Enchiladas, 58

T

Taco Braid, 82
Taco Crescents, 86
Taco-Filled Pasta Shells, 76
Taco Muffins, 79
Taco Pasta Salad, 49
Taco Pinwheels, 15
Taco Soup, 27
Tamale Pie, 75
Tamales, 68
Taquitos with Salsa, 6
Tex-Mex Bean Salad, 53
Tex-Mex Biscuits, 85
Tex-Mex Chicken Soup, 34
Tex-Mex Turkey Tacos, 67
Texas Caviar, 11
Texas Corn Chowder, 23
Texas Stew, 26
Texas Style Lasagna, 88
Texas Turkey Soup, 28
Three Milk Cake, 102
Three-Pepper Corn Pudding, 51
Tilapia with Corn Salsa, 61
Tortilla Dessert Cups, 97
Tortilla Soup, 32
Tres Leches Cake, 96

V

Vegetarian Black Bean Soup, 37
Veggie Brown Rice Wraps, 67

W

Warm Black Bean Dip, 9

Z

Zesty Cheese Soup, 27
Zesty Corn Chowder, 34
Zippy Chicken Corn Chowder, 33